CATHOLIC UTAH AT THE TURN OF THE CENTURY

1988-2002

MSGR. J. TERRENCE FITZGERALD, V.G., P.A.
BERNICE MAHER MOONEY, ARCHIVIST EMERITUS

The Catholic Diocese of Salt Lake City
Salt Lake City, Utah

Designed by Humaniz, Inc., Salt Lake City, Utah
Manufactured in the United States of America

Printed on acid-free paper
ISBN 0-9619627-2-0

TABLE OF
CONTENTS

PREFACE

Rather than a comprehensive sequel to the book, S*ALT OF THE EARTH, a History of the Diocese of Salt Lake City from 1776 – 1987*, this writing is more of a postscript, an addendum of the years 1988 through 2002. The events reported herein do not yet qualify by sufficient passage of time to be dispatched into the realm of permanent conservation; however, they are unprecedented and compelling. A sense of urgency exists to capture them somehow in the actual spirit in which they took place, and in the thoughts and words of those who engineered and lived them. Accordingly, we have collaborated to compile this chronology from the perspectives both of historical preservation and of contemporary experience.

We thank Bishop George Niederauer for his enthusiastic encouragement of our endeavor. And we express our gratitude to all who have helped us along the way. The book could not have been completed without the willing cooperation of the entire Pastoral Center staff and its varied fields of expertise, though we most often called upon Barbara Stinson Lee, editor of the *Intermountain Catholic*, and Gary Topping, diocesan archivist. Our work hopefully will enlighten history's perception of the turn-of-the-century diocese, and the heritage that it carries into the future.

Msgr. J. Terrence Fitzgerald, V.G., P.A.
Bernice Maher Mooney, Archivist Emeritus

FOREWORD

The story of the Catholic Church in each generation, in every place, is the continuing story of God's saving action among us. Catholics believe that the Son of God became man in Jesus Christ our Savior. Ever since that intersection of eternity with time, the Catholic Church has taken very seriously the way God constantly acts in and through human history.

We Catholics of Utah have been greatly blessed with the gifts and service of Msgr. J. Terrence Fitzgerald and Bernice Maher Mooney, co-authors of this addition to the history of the Catholic faith in Utah, *Salt of the Earth*, 1776-1987. This present work covers the years between 1988 and 2002, thus bringing the record of our local Church's life into the third Christian millennium.

These fourteen years were extraordinarily crowded with developments and milestones for the Diocese of Salt Lake City: in 1991, the centenary of the diocese; in 1993, the rededication of the renovated Cathedral of the Madeleine; in 1994, the transfer of Bishop William K. Weigand to Sacramento, California, and later that year, the appointment of Msgr. George Niederauer as eighth Bishop of Salt Lake City; and in 1999 the dedication of the Skaggs Catholic Center in Draper. These moments and many more are faithfully recorded in this work. Most important of all, during just these fourteen years, the number of Catholics in Utah doubled, to 200,000.

We are grateful to God for the blessings recounted here, and to each other for the gifts and sacrifices of all our people, clergy, religious and lay people alike. May the Lord continue to bless and prosper the work of the Utah Catholic Church that He has begun so richly among us.

GEORGE NIEDERAUER
Eighth Bishop of the Diocese of Salt Lake City

I

·····························

BISHOP
WILLIAM K.
WEIGAND

1988 - 1993

C onditioned by a decade of ministry in Cali, Colombia, Bishop William K.
Weigand brought to the Diocese of Salt Lake City an unprecedented focus on
ethnic diversity and social justice which inspired the extensive development
of Utah's missions. That focus, along with the interior restoration of the Cathedral of
the Madeleine, remains the definitive legacy of his presence in Utah.

BISHOP WEIGAND AND THE RESTORATION OF THE
CATHEDRAL OF THE MADELEINE

History itself mandated the cathedral restoration project: during the 90 years
since the cathedral was constructed, and the 70 years since Bishop Joseph S. Glass
had redecorated its interior, the ravages of age had grievously degraded the murals,
woodwork and windows. In 1987 Bishop Weigand set into motion the interior
restoration of the structure to honor the one hundredth anniversary of the
founding of the Diocese of Salt Lake City in 1891, and the cathedral's historical
significance as a state and national monument of spiritual strength for people of
all faiths.

Facing a daunting task of massive scope, Bishop Weigand personally directed
the project throughout, carefully nurturing the participation of both his people
and the community at large. He called upon the generous cooperation of three
co-chairmen, John W. Gallivan, Jon M. Huntsman, Sr. and Ian M. Cumming.
Msgr. M. Francis Mannion, cathedral rector and recognized liturgical scholar,
served as the campaign coordinator, guiding seemingly endless stages of planning,
and the work of steering committees studying the feasibility of a financial
projection of $6.3 million, as well as organization charts, strategies, timetables,
special events, and architectural proposals.[1]

The planning and execution of the restoration of the
interior of the Cathedral of the Madeleine extended
over a decade, but the transforming work of renovation
actually took place from 1991, when the interior was
closed to worship, until its reopening in 1993.
PHOTO BY RICHARD PREHN

Project architects, Beyer, Blinder and Belle of New York City, presented their plans for the schematic design phase of the work at the restoration inauguration reception of October 11, 1989.[2] During that same year deanery seminars energized parishioners' support as the restoration slowly took on an exciting momentum. By 1991 a major diocesan-wide campaign successfully exceeded its goal by raising $6,380,721 in pledges.[3] The importance of including an unforeseen seismic retrofit of the tower, roof and walls (the need for which became apparent after the 1990 earthquakes in San Francisco) unexpectedly added $1.8 million to already staggering costs.[4]

Finally a Hard Hat party, staged in the nave of the cathedral in 1991, launched the actual construction phase that would possess the interior for two years. By February 20, 1991, the structure was closed, scaffolding was raised, pews were being hauled out for refinishing, and already sawdust and falling plaster littered the floor. Cathedral Masses moved to the nearby public elementary Lowell School and continued there without interruption until New Year's Day, 1993. Craftsmen of the New York City firm of Rohlf's Stained and Leaded Glass Studio, Inc. dismantled the cathedral's 21 exquisite stained glass windows, piece by piece, and shipped them to Mt. Vernon, New York. There artisans cleaned off years of grime, repaired breaks and lead defects, constructed new framings, and installed a new venting system for airflow.[5] Meanwhile in Salt Lake, hollow window openings gutted the cathedral's stone walls, testifying to the temporary suspension of the usual peace and silence within the sacred shell.

Makeshift elevators, one in the interior and one outside, lifted art restorationists of Evergreene Paint Studios, Inc., also of New York, onto high platforms to retrieve the cathedral's originally magnificent murals from erosion and water damage, as well as the threat of chipped plaster and sagging canvas peeling from the walls.[6] Elsewhere in the interior, wood carvers repaired and refinished masterfully carved statues, extensive paneling, the pulpit, and ornate oak reredos behind the high altar and side chapels. Working beside them were lighting and acoustical engineers, carpenters reconfiguring pews and confessionals, artisans constructing sections of new tile flooring, and artists completing new paintings for the transept shrines and the Stations of the Cross.

Decisions made during development of the architectural design expanded the restoration program to incorporate liturgical renovations of the sanctuary, altar, and baptismal font. Thus master carver Ian Agrell of Agrell and Thorpe, Ltd. of California executed the 14-foot high wooden tabernacle in the new Blessed

On February 21, 1993, a Mass of rededication of the cathedral marked the presence of a number of visiting and local dignitaries in the sanctuary.
PHOTO BY RICHARD PREHN

Sacrament Chapel, and the 22-foot wide carved screen installed in the cathedral sanctuary.[7] An ornate octagonal baptismal font, providing both the traditional upper font and the ancient immersion font, was located symbolically, in accordance with liturgical renewal, at the entrance to the nave. The central focus of the entire interior was the altar, of Carrara onyx inlaid with glass mosaic, positioned on marble flooring in the heart of the church at the crossing of the nave and transepts.[8]

Following the rededication of the cathedral to public service on February 20, 1993, the principals of the restoration program gathered in the rectory parlor. Present were, left to right, Msgr. M. Francis Mannion, Charles Culp, Archbishop Agostino Cacciavillan, Bishop Weigand, architect John Belle, Bishop Federal, Irene C. Sweeney, Roger Cardinal Mahony and John W. Gallivan, KSG. PHOTO BY RICHARD PREHN

In November of 1989 Spencer F. Eccles and Dolores Doré Eccles toured the cathedral in anticipation of the installation of a new pipe organ for which the George S. and Dolores Doré Eccles Foundation donated $500,000. The organ, designed and built in Ireland by Kenneth Jones, was stored in the cathedral basement until its installation in the choir loft. Today the beautiful instrument of 4,066 pipes and fanfare trumpet enhances both the liturgical life of the cathedral and concert performances of the civic community.[9] The notice of the ninth annual Eccles Organ Festival, held in the fall of 2002, announced the organists who performed at five recitals open to the public free of charge, and noted that the festival is supported in part by the Utah Arts Council.

Upon the reopening of the cathedral at the end of construction in 1993, the renovated murals, woods, glass, and tile all mingled like magnificent mosaics into a breathtaking collage, brilliant in color, a stunning expression of universal faith. Bishop Weigand acknowledged the widespread religious and civic support throughout the restoration at a gathering for Rededication of the Cathedral to Public

Service on Saturday, February 20, 1993. Mass for the Dedication took place the following day, and, on Monday, Utah Chamber artists presented a concert of thanksgiving. The final cost of the restoration amounted to $9.7 million dollars, raised in part through generous contributions from corporate, foundation and religious donors, most notably the Church of Jesus Christ of Latter Day Saints, and the Episcopal Diocese of Utah. Lady Irene Sweeney and Lady Enid Cosgriff of the Equestrian Order of the Holy Sepulchre of Jerusalem were among a handful of cathedral parishioners and diocesan benefactors who were instrumental in the fundraising success.

RESTORATION LEGACY

The motto chosen for the restoration, "A Cathedral for all People," resounded in a new awareness of age-old traditions in the great cathedrals of Europe. In that same heritage the renewed Cathedral of the Madeleine generated fresh vitality in downtown Salt Lake City. The Good Samaritan program, providing food, housing and assistance for the poor, was widely expanded, as were the annual Madeleine Festival of the Arts and Humanities, the adult Choir of the Cathedral and the Madeleine Choir School.

The Good Samaritan program, successor to the Community Ministries Program established by Msgr. William H. McDougall during his tenure as cathedral rector from 1960 through 1980, mobilized a corps of volunteers who on 365 days a year prepare sack lunches. In 2002 they distributed approximately 10,000 of the lunches monthly at the cathedral door to an ever-growing number of poor and transient people of all faith traditions. Food for the meals is generously donated by the Utah Food Bank, area churches and businesses, civic groups and individual benefactors. The program's annual telethon and fund-raising dinner provide major financial support.[10]

In the spring of 1988 the cathedral sponsored the first annual Madeleine Festival of the Arts and Humanities as a service to the intellectual, artistic and cultural life of the civic community of Salt Lake. Each year the festival has presented an outstanding series of artists, lecturers and musicians in varied productions, including choral and symphony concerts. These performances in the cathedral welcome overflowing numbers, free of charge.[11] The festival is maintained largely through the annual Madeleine Award dinner, first held in March 1989, which each year honors members of the community who have contributed extensively to the arts.[12]

The Madeleine Choir School, founded in 1990 by Gregory Glenn and Msgr. M. Francis Mannion, operated in the basement of the cathedral until December 2002, when the students moved above the cathedral complex to the site of the former Rowland Hall-St. Marks School. The expanded campus enhances the distinguished achievements of the Choir School's unique academic program.
PHOTOS COURTESY OF THE INTERMOUNTAIN CATHOLIC

The Madeleine Choir School, consisting of a boys' and girls' choir, opened in the cathedral basement in 1990 as an after-school choir program, and became a full-time academic day school in August 1996. Its founder, Gregory Glenn, supported by the cathedral rector, Msgr. Mannion, envisioned the school as one that provides children with the musical skills necessary to become the singers, organists, composers, and instrumentalists of the future.[13] The student body of 2001-2002 numbered 111 students in grades 4 through 8. With ongoing enthusiastic dedication, Elizabeth Hunt, principal of the Choir School, assured the school's commitment to academic achievement along with its unique specialization in the disciplines of music and liturgy.

The Choir School assists with the worship life of the Cathedral, and has become widely recognized. It has performed in concerts with Ballet West, the Utah Symphony, Children's Dance Theater, the Mormon Tabernacle Choir, and the San Francisco Opera. The choir sang at the 2002 Olympics in Salt Lake City, and recently completed a tour of France, Belgium and Germany. In February 2003 the choristers will revisit Italy. In 1998 they were invited to sing for Pope John Paul II, and their performance for him at St. Peter's Basilica in Rome on February 1, 1998 remains one of their most memorable experiences.[14]

The generosity of many Choir School families and patrons, including Robert C. Steiner, the Thomas K. McCarthey Family, Terence K. Stephens, and the Dan Murphy Foundation, enabled acquisition in May 2002 of a new campus located on the city block at the northwest corner of the cathedral. This site, owned by the Episcopal Diocese since 1871, formerly housed Rowland Hall-St. Mark's School.[15] The support of Bishop Niederauer, and that of the newly-appointed cathedral rector, Rev. Joseph M. Mayo, was instrumental in this effort. In late 2002 the Madeleine Choir School moved to its new campus, where 167 children are currently taught in grades 2 through 8.

The cathedral's expanded outreach to the poor, and enriched programs for the arts and music education stretched the parish's financial and physical resources during the post interior-restoration years. Completion of unfinished details of the construction phase of the restoration, and maintenance of the new and restored areas, proved demanding. In the basement, school activities absorbed the parish Scanlan Hall. The rectory adjoining the cathedral fell into disrepair. The coming of the new millennium, however, energized change as the approaching 2002 Olympics inspired the interior renovation of the rectory. And the moving of the Madeleine Choir School in late 2002 to its expansive new campus relieved pressure on the cathedral complex.

CONCURRENT WITH THE CATHEDRAL RESTORATION:
DIOCESAN CENTENNIAL CELEBRATIONS AND THE
YEAR OF EVANGELIZATION

The centennial celebration of the creation of the diocese in 1891 paralleled the
process of the cathedral restoration. In 1985[16] Bishop Weigand had appointed a task
force to prepare for a period of celebration extending from November 23, 1986, the
100th anniversary of the founding of the Vicariate of Utah, through January 27,
1991, the 100th anniversary of the creation of the Diocese of Salt Lake. Completion
of the interior restoration of the cathedral would mark these centennials.

In 1986 a Centennial Steering Committee chose the diocesan coat of arms as
the centennial logo, and a centennial cross as the main symbol. "Lift High the
Cross" became the official hymn, and the slogan honored "Jesus Christ, the Same
Yesterday, Today and Forever." Pencil sketches of each parish and mission by artist
Paul Heath encouraged the rediscovery of local parish and diocesan history, and
centennial themes were incorporated into existing parish programs.[17] During 1986
and 1987 each of the five deaneries in Utah held a special Mass in celebration of
the establishment of the Vicariate of Utah in 1886.[18]

Meanwhile, a committee was established to plan and orchestrate a diocesan Year
of Evangelization from September 1990 through June 1992, which coincided with the
National Conference of Catholic Bishops' (NCCB) 1991 consultation on its National
Plan and Strategy for Catholic Evangelization in the United States. This committee
was chaired by Msgr. J. Terrence Fitzgerald, a diocesan priest who had recently
returned to the diocese after completing six years as president-rector of Mount
Angel Seminary in Oregon. Throughout the Year of Evangelization, committee members explored the concept of personal and family spiritual renewal, and worked to
provide a hospitable environment in the parishes for evangelization, which the NCCB
defined as, "bringing the Good News into all strata of culture…transforming all
things into Christ." The heightened awareness of evangelization added depth and
resolve to preparations for the approaching centennial events of 1991.[19]

During 1990 the Centennial Steering Committee sharpened its focus on myriad
details necessary to stage the main centennial events. Broad newspaper and media
coverage announcing the celebration included the widely-distributed television
documentary video, "100 Candles, Utah's Catholic Centennial."[20] Finally, on
January 27, 1991, exactly 100 years from the day on which Pope Leo XIII erected
the Diocese of Salt Lake City, a special Mass was celebrated at the cathedral, in
conjunction with a banquet held at the Red Lion Hotel the following day.

Thousands of Catholics from throughout Utah attended the official centennial Mass held on April 14, 1991 at the Jon M. Huntsman Center, University of Utah. Not only did this day mark a major highlight of Utah's Catholic history, it also honored the historical dimensions of these local events within the universal Catholic heritage. The year 1991 represented the 100th anniversary of *Rerum Novarum* (the social encyclical of Pope Leo XIII), the 500th anniversary of the birth of St. Ignatius Loyola, and the 500th anniversary of the coming of the Gospel to the Americas.

In the festive atmosphere of the Huntsman Center on April 14, large colorful banners, representing parishes from the smallest rural mission to the largest city parish, hung suspended from the ceiling. Preliminary activities spotlighted Utah's collective Catholic family as both multicultural and homogeneous. Native Americans in tribal dress transformed the platform that served as center stage into a sacred space with their solemn "Blessing of the Four Winds." Within this sanctuary stood the centennial crucifix and altar to which a dignified procession slowly wound its way amid the native music of Vietnamese, Hispanic and Tongan choirs.

Leading the procession were the Fourth Degree Knights of Columbus in regal attire, standard bearers for each deanery including representatives of Catholic cultural groups, diocesan organizations, and men and women religious, as well as seminarians, civic officials and neighbors of other faiths. Following these appeared the deacons of the day's liturgy, concelebrating priests of the diocese, and the visiting bishops.[21]

Among those concelebrating the centennial Mass with Bishop Weigand were retired Bishop Joseph Lennox Federal, the sixth bishop of the Diocese of Salt Lake City, and thirteen bishops of neighboring dioceses in the western United States. The Most Rev. John R. Quinn, Archbishop of San Francisco, was homilist for the occasion. The liturgy concluded with the reading of a personal greeting from Pope John Paul II to Bishop

At the liturgy celebrating the centennial of the Diocese of Salt Lake City on April 14, 1991, Bishop Joseph Lennox Federal was honored on the 40th anniversary of his April 11, 1951 episcopal ordination. The centennial ceremony concluded as Bishop Weigand read personal greetings from Pope John Paul II to Bishop Federal.
PHOTO COURTESY OF DIOCESAN ARCHIVES

Federal, who was simultaneously celebrating the 40th anniversary of his episcopal ordination. A prolonged standing ovation for the beloved retired bishop reflected the enthusiastic joy, pride and gratitude felt at this historical moment by Utah Catholics.

UTAH'S RURAL MINISTRIES: CATHOLIC CHURCH EXTENSION SOCIETY, AND OTHER BENEFACTORS

Between 1988 and 1993 Bishop Weigand dedicated 11 new parish and mission churches, and blessed additions to six others.

....

1988-1993:

*Formal Dedications of 11 **New** Parish and Mission Churches, and of New Additions to Six **Established** Parish or Mission Churches:*

PARISH		MISSION	
1988	St. Martin de Porres, Taylorsville	1989	Holy Family, Fillmore
1989	St. Mary, Ogden: Education Center	1989	St. Gertrude, Panguitch
1989	San Andres, Payson: Refurbished	1989	Santa Ana, Tremonton
1991	Christ the King, Cedar City	1990	Holy Family, Ogden: Parish Center
1991	St. Elizabeth, Monroe		
1991	Sts. Peter and Paul, West Valley City	1990	St. Florence, Huntsville
		1991	St. Anthony, Torrey
1992	Blessed Sacrament, Sandy: Parish Center	1991	San Felipe, Wendover
1993	Our Lady of Guadalupe, SLC: Parish Center	1991	San Rafael, Huntington: Parish Center
1993	St. Thomas More, Sandy		

The Catholic Church Extension Society, founded in the United States in 1905 to assist the struggling Catholic presence in poor missionary outposts, has consistently supported such new and expanded construction within the Diocese of Salt Lake City since the era (1915-1925) of its second bishop, Joseph S. Glass.

St. Therese of the Child Jesus parish church, Midvale, 1927, located near the present church constructed in 1974. Extension Society funds contributed to the new religious education center built in the year 2000. PHOTO COURTESY OF DIOCESAN ARCHIVES

1920-1995:

Among the parishes and missions in the Diocese of Salt Lake City that have benefited from Catholic Church Extension Society grants:

YEAR OF GRANT		YEAR OF GRANT	
1920	Notre Dame de Lourdes, Price	1951;1994	Our Lady of Lourdes, Magna
1922	St. Francis of Assisi, Provo	1952	St. Bridget, Milford
1923	St. James, Vernal	1953;1988	St. Christopher, Kanab
1923	St. Mary of the Assumption, Park City	1954	St. Francis Xavier, Kearns
1923	Good Shepherd, Garfield	1960	St. Pius X, Moab: LaSal Chapel
1926	St. Vincent de Paul, Murray	1988	Christ the King, Cedar City
1935;1988	St. Joseph, Monticello	1989	St. Michael Mission, Panguitch
1941	St. Thomas Aquinas, Logan	1990	San Felipe, Wendover
1945	Sacred Heart Chapel, Sunnyside	1995	Vietnamese Community, Kearns
1945	St. Marguerite, Tooele		
1947	St. Elizabeth, Monroe		
1948	St. Rose of Lima, Layton		
1950	St. George, St. George		

Present Notre Dame de Lourdes Church, Price, established in 1918; Father Donald E. Hope, pastor.
PHOTO COURTESY OF DIOCESAN ARCHIVES

1992-2002:

Special Projects funded by the Catholic Church Extension Society in the
Diocese of Salt Lake City:

1992	St. Mary's Home for Men, Salt Lake City	$52,000
1993	Guadalupe, Salt Lake City: Education Center	$50,000
1994	Sacred Heart, Salt Lake City: Church	$50,000
1995	Our Lady of Lourdes, Magna: Church	$20,000
1995	Our Lady of Perpetual Help, Kearns: Church	$60,000
1995	Our Lady of the Mountains Retreat House, Ogden	$20,000
1996	Notre Dame, Price: Newman/Religious Ed. Center	$20,000
1996	Immaculate Conception, Copperton: Roof	$10,000
1997	St. George, St. George: Diaconate Home	$40,000
1998	San Andres, Payson: Furnace	$ 7,000
1998	St. Bridget, Milford: Parish Hall	$10,000
1998	Good Shepherd, East Carbon: Roof and Furnace	$ 8,000
1999	St. Sylvester Mission, Escalante: Mission House	$25,000
2000	St. Therese of the Child Jesus, Midvale: Relig. Ed.	$30,000
2001	Christ the King, Cedar City: Rectory	$40,000
2001	St. Dominic Mission, Bryce Canyon: Fence	$ 5,000
2002	Beryl Junction Mission, Iron County: Mission House	$40,000

Construction of the new Christ the King Parish complex is underway to meet the needs of a rapidly growing Catholic community in Cedar City. This rectory was completed on this five-acre site in the Mesa Hills area in late 2002. Phase I of the building project will provide a new parish church, six classrooms and administrative offices. PHOTO COURTESY OF DIOCESAN ARCHIVES

Christ the King Parish, Father Michael J. Winterer, pastor; construction site of new parish church, Cedar City, Utah, 2002.
PHOTO COURTESY OF DIOCESAN ARCHIVES

The Society requires the development of a five-year plan for each qualified mission area in the United States. On March 25, 1988, Bishop Weigand was notified by Richard A. Ritter, Vice President of the Society, that, "Within the next five years the Diocese of Salt Lake City will receive grants totaling $1.25 million from the Catholic Church Extension Society. The program of $250,000 yearly for the missions in Utah began in July 1987." In the five years preceding 1988 the Society had donated over $500,000 to the diocese as direct grants for specific projects, and matching-fund grants to assist a parish or mission building effort, as well as to provide for the education of seminarians and expanded diocesan ministries.

In April 1988 the Society honored Utah's Dominican, Father Joseph A. Valine, age 90, pastor of Milford, as the year's model of the missionary spirit in the United States. "His life reflects the work of many, many priests working quietly but with grace in the rural parts of our country, "said Father Edward Slattery, president of the Extension Society. At the Society's eleventh annual award ceremony, after a special Mass in Chicago, Father Valine was honored with the prestigious "Lumen Christie Award" consisting of a bronze plaque, $2,500 for himself, and $25,000 for his diocese. Father Valine had begun his ministry in Logan, Utah in 1941, and served there as pastor from 1941 to 1946 at St. Thomas Aquinas Parish, the construction of which was largely financed by the Extension Society. In 1947 he was sent to Milford, where he labored fruitfully until his death in 1992, caring for cities and towns throughout all of southwestern Utah, including Kanab, and tourists at Grand Canyon, Zion and Bryce Canyons. To help support his ministry in the growing number of rural parishes and missions, Father Valine farmed, harvested and sold 260 acres of alfalfa each year. He worked as a caterer, and, in later years, made doughnuts to sell after Masses at his mission posts. His life of dedicated, selfless service in Utah inspires others to serve the home missions and to support the Extension Society.

The Catholic Church Extension Society has also subsidized the work of religious women, priests and deacons in rural Utah, and of campus and lay ministries development. It contributed to Utah Paulist radio program broadcasts, heard throughout the Intermountain West, and to the "Faith Alive" section of the *Intermountain Catholic* newspaper.

During the 1992-1997 grant period Father Slattery was succeeded by Msgr. Kenneth Velo as president of the Society. As diocesan administrator, Msgr. J. Terrence Fitzgerald, on March 31, 1994, submitted the extensive documentation required for the annual Grant Request, as the former vicar general, Msgr. Robert J.

Bussen, had done during Bishop Weigand's tenure. Msgr. Fitzgerald justified the needs he presented, and noted that, "The impact of the Catholic Church Extension Society on the Church in Utah is powerful. Hopefully you will continue to help our mission area."[22] A warm friendship grew between Msgr. Fitzgerald and Msgr. Velo, who personally visited Salt Lake City in 1997.

Also instrumental in support of Utah's missions are the United States Conference of Catholic Bishops' Committee on Home Missions, as well as the National Office of Black and Native Americans. Both contribute annually to the development of Utah's rural ministries. Since the era of Bishop Joseph Lennox Federal, the Lucien B. and Katherine E. Price Foundation has also distributed funds to assist Utah's missionary efforts. Current members of the board are Dr. Edward and Sheila Flanagan of Hartford, Connecticut, Msgr. Fitzgerald and Rev. Colin F. Bircumshaw.

APPOINTMENT OF BISHOP WEIGAND TO SACRAMENTO, CALIFORNIA

Less than a year after the reopening of the restored cathedral, Bishop Weigand received word of his appointment by Pope John Paul II on November 18, 1993 as bishop of Sacramento, the capital of California. A farewell Mass and an ecumenical banquet highlighted events honoring him on January 10, 1994. He left Salt Lake City amid glowing tributes from Catholics as well as from the many other friends he came to know during the cathedral restoration.

Bishop Weigand's fourteen years of episcopal leadership prepared the way for the growing diverse Catholic population that would gradually impact the state. His fundraising success, creation of the Catholic Foundation, and establishment of parishes and missions, brought notable significance to Utah's Catholics.

Except for references to non-diocesan newspapers or publications,
the Archives of the Catholic Diocese of Salt Lake City is the source of endnotes.

NOTES:

[1]   Records of the Cathedral of the Madeleine Interior Restoration/Renovation, 1987-1994,
      with finding aid, Archives, Diocese of Salt Lake City.

[2]   Ibid., Beyer, Blinder and Belle, Boxes VIII through XII.

[3]   Ibid., Box II, folder 5f.

[4]   Ibid., Box XIV, folder 36; Box XIII, folder 8.

[5]   Ibid., Box XV, folder 59.

[6]   Ibid., Box XIV, folder 37.

[7]   Ibid., Box XV, folder 60.

[8]   Ibid., Box XV, folder 40.

[9]   *Intermountain Catholic*, November 24, 1989, page 7.

[10] Ibid., November 13, 1998, page 20.

[11] Ibid., January 8, 1988, page 12; April 8, 1988, page 12.

[12] Ibid., March 31, 1989, page 3.

[13] Program, *The Choir of the Cathedral of the Madeleine Thirteenth Annual Concert Series*,
      2002-2003, page 12. Cathedral of the Madeleine, Salt Lake City.

[14] *Intermountain Catholic*, January 23, 1998, page 10; March 6, 1998, page 5.

[15] Sunday bulletin, The Cathedral of the Madeleine, July 21, 2002, page 1. For the story of the
      Episcopal Church acquisition and subsequent use of the property at this site, see Mary R. Clark,
      "Rowland Hall-St. Mark's School: Alternative Education for More than a Century,"
      Utah Historical Quarterly 48 (Summer 1980), pages 272-292.

[16] Bishop Weigand chose to make this announcement on May 10, 1985, the 70th anniversary of the
      death of Bishop Lawrence Scanlan, Utah's first Catholic bishop.

[17] Centennial Binder, Centennial Steering Committee, October 20, 1986.

[18] *The Standard Examiner*, Ogden, Utah, November 29, 1986, page 1.

[19] *Intermountain Catholic*, October 5, 1990, page 7.

[20] Records of The Cathedral of the Madeleine Interior Restoration/Renovation, Boxes IIA and IIB.

[21] Program, "Celebrating the Centennials of the Diocese of Salt Lake City," April 14, 1991.

[22] Msgr. J. Terrence Fitzgerald to Richard A. Ritter, March 31, 1994, in *Catholic Church Extension
      Society*, Box 1 of 2, "Second 5-Year Plan #2", Grant Request, page 12.

II

YEAR OF
INTERREGNUM

1994

*C*anon Law provides for interim leadership in a diocese during the time of transition of authority from a transferred diocesan bishop to that of a newly-appointed one. On January 27, 1994, the day after Bishop William K. Weigand was installed as the new bishop of Sacramento in California, the consultors of the Diocese of Salt Lake City (the priests appointed to officially advise the bishop throughout his tenure) met to choose an administrator to take the helm until a new bishop could be installed.

Among the seven consultors serving at this time were Msgr. Robert J. Bussen, Msgr. John J. Hedderman, Msgr. M. Francis Mannion, Father Thomas L. McNamara, O.S.F.S., Msgr. Robert R. Servatius and Msgr. John J. Sullivan. They elected Msgr. J. Terrence Fitzgerald, himself a consultor since 1993, and a native Utah priest for 32 years, well qualified in both pastoral and administrative experience. His term as diocesan administrator began immediately and would extend through January 25, 1995.

THE SALE OF UTAH'S CATHOLIC HOSPITALS

One of the major concerns of 1993 that came to closure during 1994, the year of interregnum, was the sale of the Holy Cross Hospitals, a matter with which Msgr. Fitzgerald and the consultors were already familiar. They had occasionally discussed the vulnerability of the hospitals, but were suddenly made aware of the critical nature of the issue on May 17, 1993 when the Congregation of the Sisters of the Holy Cross asked Bishop Weigand to approve their sale of Holy Cross Health Services of Utah (HCHSU).

The sisters had created Holy Cross Healthcare Systems (HCHS) of St. Mary's at Notre Dame, Indiana in 1979 to consolidate their Holy Cross hospitals throughout the United States, and to pool their resources. Holy Cross Healthcare

Services of Utah (HCHSU) was founded in 1987 by the sisters as a holding company for HCHS. HCHSU consisted of: 1) Holy Cross Hospital in downtown Salt Lake City, founded in 1875; 2) St. Benedict Hospital, Ogden, founded in 1946, and transferred to HCHSU by the Benedictine Sisters in 1986, given the intense competitive nature of Utah health care, and their debt; and 3) Holy Cross Jordan Valley Hospital, West Jordan, Utah, founded in 1983.

Though neither HCHS nor HCHSU was under the jurisdiction of Bishop Weigand, the Code of Canon Law mandated that "any sale of property owned by a church entity must be approved by the proper level of church authority, depending on the value of the property."[1] In their case for the sale, the sisters cited "the changing health care environment and the competitive health care market in Utah,"[2] explaining that in 1993 the Utah hospitals represented one of the weakest links in the nationwide HCHS, and were indebted "reportedly in excess of $60 million."[3]

> *No sponsor exists to assume sponsorship of HCHSU . . .*
> *we find it necessary to seek out other potential buyers . . .*
> *We are at a point in our history . . . when it seems to us*
> *that we must withdraw institutional health care presence from the area.*[4]

HCHS presented no alternatives to the proposed sale, and sought full latitude to deal with potential buyers. Though dismayed at the possible ending of the distinguished record of splendid Catholic healthcare in Utah by the Holy Cross and Benedictine Sisters for 118 years and 47 years, respectively, as well as the impact the sale would have throughout the state, Bishop Weigand and his consultors had to confront realities. The east wing of the downtown Holy Cross Hospital required massive capital improvement; in fact, "The plan to infuse over $100 million into the HCHSU for updating would put the entire HCHS at risk."[5] Further, it was known that "Health care analysts feel that, standing alone, the Holy Cross facilities are in a weak position to compete against health care giants . . . which dominate the Wasatch Front."[6]

Though "reluctantly sympathetic,"[7] Bishop Weigand signed his approval of the sisters' request, two days following receipt of their letter, after emphasizing that every effort be made to locate a Catholic system to take over the Utah hospitals. The Vatican Congregation for Institutes of Consecrated Life then granted the indult, the required official approval, on June 18, 1993.

The following September 30, 1993, HCHS unexpectedly notified Bishop Weigand that in mid-September they had signed a letter of intent to sell HCHSU to HealthTrust, Inc., a for-profit commercial entity based in Nashville, Tennessee, and the parent company of HealthTrust-Utah. In effect, the disturbing news was that "HCHS and HealthTrust, Inc. have entered into an exclusive intent to buy/sell HCHSU, and are currently involved in a sixty-day process of 'due diligence.'"[8] HCHSU was thus bound to exclusivity, confidentiality and collaboration for the defined period of time, and was subject to legal penalties for any breach of this commitment.

Bishop Weigand responded vigorously. He had become aware that a Catholic not-for-profit buyer, Sisters of Charity Healthcare System (SCH) of Houston, Texas, might possibly consider the purchase, provided legal complexities of the letter of intent could be resolved. After consultation with a group of prominent Utah laity, he asked the Sacred Congregation on October 12 to rescind the indult, or at least temporarily suspend it, in order to provide time for exploring potential options. He traveled to Rome on October 27, 1993 to confer with His Eminence Eduardo Cardinal Martinez Somalo of the Sacred Congregation for Institutes of Consecrated Life, who then delegated the Apostolic Pro-Nuncio to the United States, Archbishop Agostino Cacciavillan, to act as intermediary in this matter.

On his return trip from Rome, the bishop met with the Holy Cross Sisters and their council in South Bend. The following day he stopped in Washington, D.C. to talk with Archbishop Cacciavillan, who, after conversations with the HCHS on November 1, did suspend the indult for thirty days. Bishop Weigand and Sister Catherine O'Brien, CSC, President of the Congregation of Sisters of the Holy Cross, traveled to Nashville on November 17 to confer for two hours with officials of HealthTrust, Inc., the parent company of HealthTrust-Utah. But it became increasingly obvious that the "due diligence" process continued to move forward on schedule, and HealthTrust, Inc. stated that it anticipated closing on the prescribed date.[9] One week later efforts at stopping the proposed sale ended abruptly.

Archbishop Cacciavillan informed both the bishop and HCHS on November 23 that in the past several weeks he had considered all "spiritual-moral, pastoral, social, legal and financial aspects" of their concerns. "I am of the opinion," he declared, "that the best course of action is to proceed with the proposed sale, and for this I remove the previous suspension of the Holy See's indult."[10] Shortly thereafter, HealthTrust, Inc. and HCHS issued a joint statement saying that in the next week they expected to complete the transaction[11] thought to amount to $140 million. HealthTrust, Inc. pledged to continue to finance charity health care in the community as the Catholic hospitals had done in the past. This mitigated the fear that the historical Catholic commitment to the poor and needy at the hospitals would discontinue.[12] Sister Patricia Vandenberg, CSC, President and Executive of HCHS, defended HCHS' search for a Catholic buyer: "In the identification and qualification of potential purchasers, we engaged nationally prominent, experienced investment banks and canonical and legal advisors."[13]

Public reaction to the reality of losing the hospitals brought widespread disbelief at first, and then an overwhelming sadness reflected in the bishop's own response, "(This) is the end of a glorious era and we cannot but grieve deeply."[14] Some generously supportive religious and civic benefactors, attracted by HCHSU's mission of accepting any patient regardless of religious affiliation or ability to pay, were unhappily caught by surprise at the news.[15] One group opposing the sale hoped, unsuccessfully, to affiliate the hospitals with another area hospital, thus strengthening the stance of all in the volatile healthcare market. This effort did not materialize.

> Bishop Weigand moved toward healing. He acknowledged that,
> *I have to respect the painful decision that was made . . . The sisters will*
> *continue a Catholic healthcare presence in Utah through the Holy Cross*
> *and St. Benedict Foundations, which will fund certain services for special or*
> *vulnerable clienteles. Some of these are already set, in accordance with the*
> *restricted nature of some donations. Others will be carefully discerned as*
> *time passes.*[16]

Meanwhile, the Federal Trade Commission (FTC), which had previously reviewed the proposed HealthTrust, Inc. purchase of HCHSU, held up the sale. The commission sought to avoid the exclusive monopoly of one healthcare provider over others, and to foster competition. It declared that HealthTrust, Inc. must include in the transaction a signed consent order, and a hold-separate agreement with the FTC. The agreement would require HealthTrust, Inc. to divest of the downtown Holy Cross Hospital, the "flagship facility" of the HCHSU, and five of its related clinics, to an independent owner, from outside of the Intermountain area, within six months of the purchase of HCHSU. Thus, after the six-month period, only St. Benedict Hospital and Holy Cross Jordan Valley, along with five HCHSU clinics, would be retained by HealthTrust, Inc.[17]

Six months later the FTC mandate was fulfilled, and Msgr. Fitzgerald, as diocesan administrator, issued a press release on June 13, 1994:

> We are pleased to learn that a determination has been made regarding the future of the three Catholic hospitals in Utah. It is our hope that the proposed course of action will benefit the people of Utah, especially the most vulnerable. We are forever grateful to the Sisters of the Holy Cross and the Sisters of St. Benedict for the fine health care ministry they have provided for so many years.

The process of healing had been slow. Msgr. Fitzgerald hoped that this closure of the sale transaction would encourage all to accept the inevitable, support the diversification of competitive health care in the community, and collaborate with the sisters in their future apostolates.[18]

Commemorative services were held at the Cathedral of the Madeleine on August 21, 1994 to honor the ministry provided by the sisters and a progression of dedicated priest-chaplains, physicians, nurses, medical staff and volunteers, as well as benefactors and community leaders. The religious who had served at the hospitals came from around the country to participate in the Sunday afternoon event. Msgr. Fitzgerald, a long-time friend of the Holy Cross Sisters, represented the diocese, and welcomed all who were present. "It is fitting that we gather here in this cathedral," he said, noting that Utah's first diocesan bishop, Lawrence Scanlan, lies buried within the cathedral.

> In 1875, nearly 120 years ago, he pleaded with the Holy Cross Sisters at Saint Mary's, Indiana, to send religious women to this wilderness, in the shadows of the beautiful Wasatch slopes, to care for the sick, and educate the people . . . This Cathedral has been significant in the life of Holy Cross Health Care. It was here that the nurses, after their grand march down South Temple, gathered to receive their pins, caps and diplomas. It was here that we gathered for the final farewell of great nurses, doctors, staff and for Holy Cross Sisters who died in Utah. It was here that we paid tribute to the Holy Cross Sisters on the Centenary of their service in our State . . .
> Holy Cross provided opportunities for women when few professional jobs were open to them. The care the sisters provided for the poor and minorities, for those who had nowhere else to go with their sick babies,

pregnant wives, black housekeepers, undocumented Mexican relative, or
friend stricken with AIDS--that care was truly compassionate. The food
and clothing the sisters handed out at the back of the hospital saved many
a family. The welcome the sisters offered to our priests, sometimes sick
in body and often discouraged in spirit, when there were no other
resources, is legendary. Holy Cross defined compassionate quality care
for us in Utah.

Msgr. Fitzgerald added that now "with the inevitable pain of closure" come
new opportunities and challenges.

Today we pray that all the sisters accomplished will live on in our hearts and
we look forward to new beginnings with Holy Cross Ministries of Utah . . .
Catholic Community Services will be working with the sisters . . . to assure a
diocesan church involvement in meeting future community needs. That was
the way it all started with Bishop Scanlan's invitation to the sisters 120
years ago. [19]

He thanked the sisters for their "120 years of congregational witness to the
healing ministry of Jesus." Speaking for the Congregation of the Sisters of the
Holy Cross were Sister Catherine O'Brien, CSC, President of the Congregation,
and Sister Patricia Vandenberg, CSC, President of the Healthcare System, who
expressed their intention to move forward with new forms of service for the
Church. This gathering marked a sad but reflective moment of bringing closure
to a distinguished chapter of Utah history.

In Ogden, the Benedictine Sisters, hospital staff, volunteers and benefactors
gathered in front of the hospital at noon on August 25, 1994, around the central
pylon depicting the motto of St. Benedict. Sister Stephanie Mongeon, OSB acted
as master of ceremonies for the "changing of the guard" from St. Benedict Hospital
to HealthTrust-Utah. Msgr. Fitzgerald recalled the role of the Benedictine Sisters
and their health system in the growth of the diocese. Sister Francis Forster, OSB
related how the good work of the hospital lived on in the lives of those who had
been touched; and Dr. Harold Vonk, M.D. spoke of the love the medical staff had
for the sisters. Les Beard of HealthTrust-Utah committed the new administration
to reverence for the traditions received from the Benedictines. Each of the sisters
was given a corsage; and, following prayer near the statue of Mary, there was a
social. Amidst tears and warm embraces, the crowd quietly disbursed.

In discussions with Archbishop Cacciavillan, Bishop Weigand had determined certain covenants to be included in the sale agreement for legal and moral protection of the sisters and the diocese. One of these mandated that the new entities could no longer use the Holy Cross or St. Benedict names or logos. Likewise, within ten days all Catholic signs and symbols at the hospitals were to be removed so as not to give the false perception that the sisters or the Church still had any ethical or legal control. The change in the names and logos, the dismantling of the chapels, relocation of all religious artifacts, and the discontinuation of weekend Masses, confirmed the grim finality of Catholic ownership of the hospitals. These changes, and the reality they signified, were especially difficult for religious, clergy and lay people. General statuary and chapel artifacts from the Holy Cross and Jordan Valley facilities were donated to Catholic Community Services for its new chapel, and to the new Vietnamese church, Our Lady of Perpetual Help. Another covenant determined that any Benedictine or Holy Cross Sisters working in the hospitals, and wishing to continue to do so, were to be given employment preference.[20]

The St. Benedict and the Holy Cross Foundation monies were not included in the sale but were to remain in Utah for community service. Out of the appreciable net proceeds of the sale, HCHSU would give the Benedictines funds to assist with their continuing Utah ministries; and HealthTrust, Inc. would contribute $1 million to the Benedictine Sisters. The sisters would continue to oversee the St. Benedict Foundation. The Holy Cross Sisters would establish a Utah "outreach to the poor," using monies from their Hospital Foundation and some funds from the sale. Thus was created today's Holy Cross Ministries, a network providing social services for the poor, especially minorities, of Utah.

Ethical values, as well as chaplaincy programs, became moot issues in the covenants with the successive sale of downtown Holy Cross Hospital.[21] However, the fifteen years of pastoral care provided by Father Matthew O. Wixted until 1989 were continued by a Catholic chaplaincy presence in the person of Father David L. Van Massenhove until his transfer to a parish in 2002. The Salt Lake hospital changed hands from HealthTrust, Inc. to Columbia Health Care of Houston in 1994, to Champion Health Care of Houston in 1995, to the merged Champion and Paracelsus in 1996, and from Paracelsus to IASIS (Greek word for healing) Health Care of Franklin, Tennessee on October 8, 1999.

Nearly a decade has gone by since Utah's Catholic hospitals passed into history; but the healing Christ-like ministry of the Holy Cross and Benedictine Sisters endures in the hearts and memories of those they served in body and in soul, many from birth until death. Throughout the West, women trained in the sisters' schools of nursing continued their tradition of quality, compassionate care.

CHRISTUS ST. JOSEPH VILLA, SALT LAKE CITY

While the people of Utah grieved the loss of its Catholic hospitals, there was great satisfaction in the growth and impact of St. Joseph Villa. The year of the interregnum, 1994, marked a turning point in the work of the Sisters of Charity of the Incarnate Word at the Villa. This order of nursing sisters had originally been founded in 1866 by the Most Reverend Claude Mary Dubuis (1817-1895), second bishop of Galveston, Texas. Seeing the need for hospitals in Houston, he told the sisters, "Our Lord Jesus Christ suffering in the persons of a multitude of the sick and the infirm of every kind seeks relief at your hands."[1] When Bishop Duane G. Hunt, fifth bishop of the diocese of Salt Lake City, invited the sisters to open a home for the aged in Utah, Mother M. Elizabeth, CCVI, replied on August 26, 1946, that "Our council members are quite willing to take up the work of caring for the aged in Salt Lake City . . . I explained to the members the manner of support we may expect—State aid and that of other charitable agencies . . . "[2]

The sisters' work in Utah for the first four decades emphasized development of the physical facility of their not-for-profit corporation of healing ministry to the elderly, including the disadvantaged and under-served of the Salt Lake City area. They cared for 15 aged residents in the former Moroni Heiner home purchased by the Congregation of the Sisters of Charity of the Incarnate Word in 1947. The clientele expanded to 76 guests with a new addition, dedicated on June 7, 1959 on the same site; and to 175 when 51 units designed for residential care were completed in a new adjoining wing during 1984.

By 1988, however, their vision for the Villa broadened to concentrate on a "holistic program, (caring for) the total person in an ecumenical and pluralistic atmosphere . . . mindful of stewardship of our resources, sensitivity to health needs of the community and cooperation with other health care providers."[3] Out of this vision came the appointment in 1987 of Richard G. Erick, an employee for thirteen years, as the first lay administrator, and of Sr. Ambrose Naughton, CCVI, who had come to the Villa the previous year, as its first executive director. On August 15, 1987 the sisters dedicated an arboretum on the grounds in celebration of the 40th anniversary of their presence at the Villa.

In March of 1988 new Articles of Incorporation and Bylaws of the Villa were drawn up, and the first assistant administrator, and a chief financial officer were appointed. The sisters elected new board members for the voluntary board of directors, which then included, besides the sisters, Bishop William K. Weigand, retired Bishop Joseph Lennox Federal as an *ex officio* member, Mr. Gordon Wilson and concerned individuals from the local community. Newly organized efforts included a Values Committee to integrate Christian values into every aspect of ministry, certification courses for nursing assistants, and programs of quality assurance and continuing education.[4]

Networking with the Diocesan Task Force on AIDS in 1988, the Villa sponsored Utah's first home for residents with AIDS, the Shalom Apartments, with nine residents who either had no place to live or limited ability to rent housing. The project was overseen by a board including, besides the sisters and the diocese, Catholic Community Services, Holy Cross Hospital, the Episcopal Diocese of Utah, and AIDS Project, Utah.[5]

Prior to the diocesan centennial celebration of 1991, Sister Ambrose reported that, "As the diocese prepares to enter its second century . . . St. Joseph Villa is expanding its vision of serving the Incarnate Word in the elderly." She would become the moving force behind a major new Continuum of Care addition to the Villa in 1995. Much of the groundwork for two new buildings and the six new services they housed would be well underway during the year of interregnum, 1994. With the continual support and collaboration of Msgr. Fitzgerald, diocesan administrator and a member of St. Joseph Villa Board of Directors, Sister Ambrose brought to reality innovative plans to dramatically restructure the Villa's not-for-profit services for the elderly of the community.

Two new buildings under construction during 1994 would house six new programs, including 60 independent-living apartments offering the security of medical and social services; and 37 assisted living quarters in a supportive residential environment. Quinney Transition Care would consist of 24 beds in 12 semi-private rooms for inpatient Medicare-certified rehabilitative therapies. Special Care would provide a home for people with Alzheimer's and related dementia in 18 private rooms in a secure supervised setting. The Adult Day Center was licensed for a capacity of 50, to promote quality of life and independence five days a week. A Senior Clinic and Mental Health Services would be opened by Intermountain Health Care for Villa residents and those in the surrounding community.[6]

On April 22, 1998 Bishop Niederauer and Sister Aloysius Mannion, CCVI of CHRISTUS St. Joseph Villa, presented the Continuum of Care Humanitarian Award to President and Mrs. Thomas S. Monson of the Church of Jesus Christ of Latter-day Saints in honor of the Monsons' generous ecumenical support for the Villa Continuum of Care program.

PHOTOS COURTESY OF THE DESERET NEWS

The Continuum of Care functions under the auspices of CHRISTUS St. Joseph Villa, though a number of its programs are supported by the contributions of community partners. The blessing and dedication of the Continuum of Care highlighted the grand opening ceremony of April 12, 1995. Bishop Niederauer, installed as the eighth bishop of the diocese the previous January 25, joined Sister Ambrose, and Galen Ewer, now Administrator/CEO of the Villa, as well as other officials, in the ribbon cutting ceremony. The invocation was delivered by Elder John E. Fowler, Second Quorum of the Seventy, Church of Jesus Christ of Latter-day Saints, representing benefactors of various faiths. The Most Rev. Joseph A. Fiorenza, bishop of the Galveston/Houston Diocese, and long-time advocate for the Incarnate Word community, came to Salt Lake for the program and offered the closing benediction. The project's extensive list of donors--county and state programs; family, corporate and religious foundations; professional and charitable institutions and organizations, as well as individuals--reflected the generous ecumenical cooperation within the Continuum of Care project.

The following month, the annual Hope for the Elderly benefit at Little America Hotel in Salt Lake City garnered support for the Villa Charity Care Fund, founded by Sister Ambrose to assure that no resident would be denied care because of lack of resources.[7] The benefit recognizes specific dedication and service within the community-wide system of volunteer contribution to the Villa. Members of one group, the Villa Volunteers, first met on May 2, 1959 and have continued to serve daily in some phase of volunteer assistance since that time.[8]

In early 1997 Bishop Niederauer officially opened the golden jubilee year of the Sisters of Charity of the Incarnate Word. The celebration at the Villa took place on the feast day of St. Joseph, March 19, 1997. Incarnate Word Sisters who had previously served in Salt Lake City gathered from throughout the country to join the Villa staff and extended family in joyful celebration of the founding and growth of St. Joseph Villa. "Over the years," Sister Ambrose stated, "our ministry has been made possible through the love and support of clergy and religious, and through the services rendered by administrative leadership and co-workers alike."[9]

Sister Ambrose, meanwhile, had been diagnosed with cancer, and in 1997, reluctantly retired to Houston. She died there on April 13, 1998 at the age of 73. Bishop Federal, then 88 years old and a resident of the Villa for three years, knowing Sister's unique courage and spiritual strength, memorialized her legacy: "She was especially instrumental in increasing the capacity of St. Joseph Villa and so increased its value to the whole community."[10] Bishop Federal followed her in death on August 31, 2000.

To further extend the healing ministry of Christ, the sisters formed the co-sponsored system, CHRISTUS HealthCare, by joining together, in February 1999, their two separate healthcare systems, the Sisters of Charity of the Incarnate Word Healthcare System (SCH) of Houston, and the Incarnate Word Healthcare System (IWHS) of San Antonio. The alliance allowed the two cousin congregations, who shared the same history and ideals, "to ensure that their mission and ministry would remain strong and viable in an ever-changing health care arena."[11]

During 1999 the Adult Day Center, opened at the Villa in 1995, moved to a new location at 2155 South 400 East. Ground had been broken at this site, on land designated by St. Ann Parish and Kearns-St. Ann School, on the previous

November 11, 1998, for a child day care center to be used by the Villa, parish and school staffs, and residents of the neighborhood. The center was named the CHRISTUS St. Joseph Villa Uarda Smart Wright Day Center. Uarda Smart Wright was a Villa resident and life-long friend of four of the families whose foundations assisted in the funding of the center. The Adult Day Center and the child day program were thus housed together in a new Intergenerational Center, which provides a unique state-licensed day program for seniors and children. Although both groups have their own areas designed for their specific needs, the two groups do meet together daily for programmed activities, allowing for intermingling and interaction between the children and the seniors.[12]

The CHRISTUS Marian Center opened in September 2002 at the Villa to offer short-term inpatient, as well as structured outpatient, behavioral health services for persons over 55 years of age. The licensed center is the only one of its kind in Salt Lake Valley with its geriatric focus on such issues as prescription drug interactions, stress, grief or depression. The program provides a secure environment in a comfortable home-like setting.[13] Today CHRISTUS St. Joseph Villa remains on the cutting edge of holistic care, continuing its outstanding healing ministry with dedication, compassion and justice, ever mindful of the resident as an integral part of its mission, and of the community as friend and collaborator.

CATHOLIC COMMUNITY SERVICES (CCS)

Catholic Community Services (CCS) was known as Catholic Charities when first formally organized in 1945 as the adjunct arm of charity within the Diocese of Salt Lake City. Its mission gradually broadened into the entire range of social services to meet Utah's needs. The name of Catholic Charities changed to CCS in 1981 to better reflect its mission. In 1994, the CCS board and administrators developed an Agency Strategic Plan with the theme, "Proclaim Justice . . . Embrace Charity." The plan defined CCS as a United Way member agency and a child welfare and placement agency licensed by the Utah State Department of Social Services.[1] It seeks to serve any man, woman or child in need, regardless of age, race, ethnic origin or creed.

On October 28, 1995, CCS observed the 50th anniversary of its founding. At the dinner celebrating the golden anniversary, 800 guests from the Salt Lake area raised $75,000 to contribute to CCS programs. The agency honored United Way and the Utah Division of Community Development as its partners in "bringing wholeness to the broken." Bishop Joseph Lennox Federal had noted, twenty years earlier, that in 1975, "CCS is funded chiefly by the United Way although it has received some support from other sources including the Diocesan Development Drive."[2]

The 50th anniversary ceremony also commended two dedicated social work leaders: Msgr. J. Terrence Fitzgerald, diocesan liaison for Catholic Charities from 1970 through 1982, and twice executive director; and Rev. Terence M. Moore, coordinator, Utah Catholic Refugee Resettlement during 1982, and executive director of CCS from July 1987 through December 1993.[3] Both retained a close relationship with CCS over the years, carefully guiding the effectiveness and accountability of its programs. The mission of CCS, in the spirit of the Gospel and Vatican II, responded over the years to the changing needs of the poor. There was greater interaction with other service providers within the community in order to better serve the vulnerable populations with the aim of assisting them to self-sufficiency.

The administration of CCS programs was housed in the old red Chancery building on South Temple from 1945 until 1987, except for the several years in the late 1970s when it was located at 2862 South State Street. In 1987 expansion of the work of CCS, and limitations of space, forced the relocation of three of its major programs–Refugee Resettlement, Referral and Family Assistance, and the Utah Immigration Project. The programs moved to the former Bishop Glass School and Convent on Goshen Street at Fourth South and Tenth West in Salt Lake City. The separate sites provided unwieldy communication between these programs and their administrators for two years, until an unexpected miracle in late 1989.

That year G. Frank Joklik, president and chief executive officer of Kennecott Corporation, which "had been part of the community most of the century," announced that Kennecott would present a "building and the land on which it stands to Catholic Community Services, a United Way agency." He added, "Catholic Community Services reflects the quality of service to others that we highly respect and regard." The Deed of Gift read:

> *In acknowledgement and appreciation of the services provided by Catholic Community Services of the State of Utah, Kennecott Corporation hereby gives, as a gift to Catholic Community Services, the Utah non-profit organization, all rights of title to the real property located at 2300 West 1700 South, Salt Lake City.*[4]

The two-story office building of 26,000 square feet on 3.45 acres of land, formerly a division of Kennecott corporate offices, provides space for centralized administration of all present CCS operations, and a strategic location for more efficient distribution of services. Clients who come to the offices are better served in more pleasant and private surroundings. Bishop William K. Weigand expressed the prayerful gratitude of the Catholic community to Kennecott Corporation when he was presented the keys to the building at an October 31, 1989 ceremony. CCS held an open house on February 22, 1990, and moved its varied operations into the new rooms over the following months.[5] Msgr. Fitzgerald formally dedicated Holy Family Chapel in the CCS building on October 7, 1994 during the year of interregnum.[6] The new altar and statuary were gifts from the former Holy Cross Hospitals.

On January 10, 1992, CCS received another stunning act of generosity: Jon M. and Karen Huntsman donated $1 million to fund an endowment for CCS' St. Vincent de Paul Center located on West Second South in Salt Lake City. Jon M. Huntsman, founder and chief executive officer of Huntsman Chemical, stated that the gift was given to St. Vincent de Paul as a permanent fund, "the earnings of which will be directed each year to assist in feeding our fellow men and women who are 'hungered.'" In his expressions of heartfelt appreciation within the Catholic community, Bishop Weigand noted that the Huntsmans have been consistently generous to CCS over the years, and that the earnings from this newly-established fund would enable the day-to-day running of the center at a time of need and strained resources.[7]

This St. Vincent de Paul Center, and the adjoining William K. Weigand Resource Center, reflect the spirit and mission of CCS today. With the help of volunteers from Catholic parishes throughout the diocese, and people of other faiths, the Soup Kitchen at St. Vincent de Paul Center regularly serves some 700 hot meals per day for six days a week during summer, and well over 900 during cold winter days. The 11,000 square foot Weigand day Resource Center was funded through the generosity of Mr. and Mrs. Sam Skaggs and the ALSAM Foundation. It was named after Bishop Weigand as a tribute to his care for the poor. The center was dedicated by Bishop Niederauer on December 15, 1995.

Here the homeless find storage for their sparse belongings, mail delivery service, showers, a laundry facility, haircuts, basic health care, a library, job listings, and emergency assistance. Day care for the children of the homeless is also provided. A huge, bright colored mural, called "Landscape of Life," looking down on the courtyard of the Weigand Resource Center, symbolizes the creativity and community sharing made possible for the homeless. Those from the St. Vincent de Paul Center, and students of the Weigand Resource HeadStart program, painted the mural along with the residents of Salt Lake City's *The Road Home* homeless shelter across the street.[8]

Additional CCS services associated with St. Vincent de Paul include transitional housing for women with children at Marillac House, and for expectant mothers at Villa Maria. CCS cooperates with other care-givers in maintaining homes both for Women's Substance Abuse, and for men rebuilding their lives at St. Mary's Home. Other CCS ministries address adoption, foster care, social and aging needs of the older adult, job training and placement for students, Kidstart for homeless children, and the "Booked Program-Library Behind Bars."

In collaboration with CCS is Holy Cross Ministries, established to assist Utah's poor by the Holy Cross Sisters after the sale of their hospitals. Sister Suzanne Brennan, CSC is executive director of Holy Cross Ministries, which offices in the CCS complex. The sisters also administer Holy Cross Welcome Center for Women, and provide additional health, education, immigration and home visiting programs for women, children, the elderly and minority groups who are at high risk and underserved throughout Utah.

CCS opened a field office at Ogden in 1982 with a local advisory board to provide essential community involvement.[9] Since 1997 CCS has maintained a food warehouse in Ogden for the poor, unemployed and ill of the area. Funds come from the Utah Food Bank, the U. S. Department of Agriculture commodities program and other donations.[10] The Ogden CCS field office also operates transitional housing to assist families working toward self-sufficiency, and a Shelter-Plus home for victims of HIV/AIDS. Various churches in the Ogden area collaborate to support St. Anne Center for the poor.

In coordination with national Catholic Relief Services, CCS offers major local programs of immigration, naturalization, and refugee foster care and resettlement. The Refugee Foster Care Program, for unaccompanied refugee youth fleeing danger and persecution, was the only such program in Utah and the Intermountain West when CCS first opened it in 1979. About 150 refugees from Kosovo were settled by CCS in Utah during 1999, and nearly 500 others from Africa, East Asia, Europe, Latin America and the Near East. Community cooperation supplements funding. For example, a KSL Radio fundraiser netted $10,000 toward refugee housing, food, clothing, and job development services. Mentors, friends and advisors also help the refugees, and Intermountain Health Care has generously treated emotionally traumatized refugee children.[11]

Especially dramatic is the story of the Lost Boys of Sudan, aged 19 through 25 who ran away at ages 5 to 8, fleeing destroyed homes and families, and fearing for their lives. They survived four years in an Ethiopian refugee camp and nine years in a Kenja camp. Most belong to the Dinka tribe, a Christian people, which the Sudanese government reportedly brutally persecutes. Case workers of the U. S. Immigration and Naturalization Service found these boys in refugee camps and brought them to the care of CCS in Utah. The boys, now young adults, seek citizenship and self-reliance. A few dream of salvaging something of their homeland in the future.[12] The Sharehouse at the offices of CCS plays a crucial role in collecting essential home furnishings and household items to support incoming refugees and, in fact, to assist all of the CCS programs.

Following the retirement of Sr. Margo Cain, CSC, as executive director of CCS (1994 to 1999), and a period of interim leadership, Maggie St. Clare, former KSL vice president for community affairs, was appointed executive director on February 1, 2002.[13] She accepted an award for the agency from the Freedom Foundation of Utah on March 22, 2002 recognizing CCS for its effort "on behalf of the poor and marginalized in Utah, those who are served by its 18 social programs." At the award ceremony, radio commentator Don Gale called CCS workers "heroes," adding that "CCS works diligently to make a difference in our society one neighbor at a time."[14]

The plunge in the stock market and the terrorist attacks of September 11, 2001 thrust CCS into an unprecedented financial crisis. Formerly reliable foundation and corporate funding was derailed in a faltering national economy, further weakened by corporate investment scandals and losses. Donations fell into a downward spiral. "It was our worst year ever," said Maggie St. Clare of the 2001-2002 fiscal year ending June 30. CCS eliminated fifteen staff positions to supplant a budget shortfall, and in February 2002 discontinued a family counseling program.[15]

In accordance with its long tradition, however, CCS perseveres in its efforts to serve the entire spectrum of Utah's social needs. The name of Catholic Community Services shall remain synonymous with "charity," both given and received. The support of the greater Utah community for its mission is remarkable.

The 11,000 sq. ft. Weigand Resource Center, a gift of the ALSAM Foundation, was named after Bishop William K. Weigand in tribute to his concern for the homeless. On December 15, 1995 Bishop Niederauer dedicated the center, where day care for children of the homeless is provided, as well as health care and emergency assistance. PHOTOS COURTESY OF DIOCESAN ARCHIVES

CATHOLIC FOUNDATION OF UTAH (CFU)

The Catholic Foundation of Utah was created under the corporate authority of Bishop William K. Weigand, seventh bishop of the diocese, on November 7, 1984.[1] Anticipating the future needs of the Church in Utah with foresight, the foundation assures and safeguards the consistent fiscal stability of the diocese. The foundation was incorporated in the State of Utah on December 31, 1992.[2] CFU Bylaws, originally written in 1985, were revised in 1993.

An executive committee, of which Bishop George Niederauer is chairman, and a board of distinguished trustees, meet quarterly to set policy and enhance the work of the foundation. Included in the agenda of the board are its careful monitoring of investment performance to ensure security and growth, and its provision of subsidy for many ministries of the diocese. The business of CFU is conducted by its executive director, Kurt Simpson, hired in 1991 from the Archdiocese of Milwaukee.

The following have served as presidents of the foundation:

Harry Isbel	1985-1986	Jack Klepinger	1992
Robert Evans	1987-1988	Dan Sample	1993-1994
William Brennan	1989-1990	Nancy Giles	1995-1997
Edward Sweeney	1991	Irene Sweeney	1998-2000
		Virginia(Ginni) Albo	2001-2003

CFU represents an important means by which current and potential donors can support the Catholic Church in the state of Utah. Bishop Niederauer noted that endowment funds "provide vital long-term security for parish communities, Church agencies and programs. The principal portion of an endowed fund is protected and nourished, indefinitely, to provide a lasting stream of income that will benefit a Church that will serve even our children's grandchildren."[3]

Juan Diego Catholic High School at the Skaggs Catholic Center, 2002. PHOTO COURTESY OF THE INTERMOUNTAIN CATHOLIC

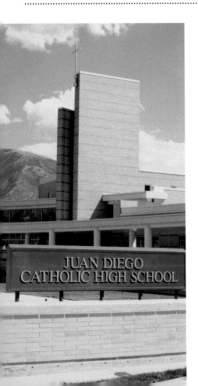

"CFU receives and manages three general types of funds:

1) Endowment funds, wherein gift restrictions designate the principal to be invested and only income is used;

2) Term endowment funds, wherein the donor has provided that the principal may be used in certain cases or after a stated period of time;

3) Unrestricted funds, available for immediate and direct program support, as well as support for CFU operations and liabilities."[4]

Charitable gifts include named family funds, and health or social services funds, as well as funds for parishes, schools, youth and seminarians.[5] Such gifts grow out of a concept of stewardship, and a prudent long-range vision of the future. "It is in the midst of our daily teaching, ministering, prayers and service, that our faith calls us to pause and dream of the future so that we might prepare to hand down the traditions and blessings of the Church to those who will come after us."[6]

Founding benefactors, Sam and Aline Skaggs, at the 1999 dedication of the Skaggs Catholic Center.
PHOTO COURTESY OF THE INTERMOUNTAIN CATHOLIC

SKAGGS CATHOLIC CENTER

At the time of the ordination of Bishop George Niederauer as eighth bishop of the diocese on January 25, 1995, a miracle was in the making. The Catholic school principals had prepared a white paper outlining the future needs of Catholic education in Utah. A priority recommendation was a future high school in the south end of the Salt Lake Valley, and additional elementary schools. After consultation, Bishop Niederauer approved the effort to purchase the abandoned Jordan High School building for a Catholic high school. The effort to purchase failed, and then the miracle unfolded.

Mr. Sam Skaggs heard of the growing demand for a Catholic high school in the south Salt Lake Valley from employees at his American Stores, and of the unsuccessful efforts of the diocese to acquire the old Jordan High building. He contacted the diocese with an offer to finance the building of a new Catholic high school. Msgr. J. Terrence Fitzgerald became the liaison, as he had long been familiar with Mr. Skaggs who had been a generous contributor to Catholic Community Services, Judge Memorial Catholic High School, and through scholarship funding by the Skaggs Family Foundation for Roman Catholic and Community Charities.

St. John the Baptist Church, Father Terence M. Moore, pastor; construction at the Skaggs Catholic Center, 2003.
PHOTO COURTESY OF DIOCESAN ARCHIVES

In time the vision for the high school expanded to include elementary and middle schools, day care, land for a future parish, and in general a center to house diocesan celebrations. As word spread of the exciting news, jubilant thanksgiving and renewed hope rippled through the diocese. The final cost of the Skaggs Catholic Center was $56 million dollars financed by Sam and his wife, Aline. This sum included the land, security, furnishings and state-of-the-art technology for all three schools.

Msgr. Fitzgerald, appointed vicar general by Bishop Niederauer in 1995, oversaw the planning, design and construction of the project. Collaborating with him was Dr. Galey Colosimo, an experienced and dedicated educator in the diocesan school system. The two traveled throughout the United States studying the components of school design, structure and ambience, searching for the best possible examples to meet the educational needs of the diocese. Their goal was a facility that would reflect the glorious tradition of Catholic education. Catholic faith life, identity, and sacramentality would be inherently visible. They used as a model the Benedictine monastic schools, centered on community life, worship, study and service. Abbot Nathan Zodrow, OSB, of Mount Angel Abbey and Seminary in Western Oregon, served as an artistic and educational consultant for the project. Bishop Niederauer's lifelong commitment to education, specifically the humanities, provided valuable insight for the endeavor.

In 1996 Sam Skaggs identified and purchased 57 acres of alfalfa fields in Draper as the site of the schools. It seemed at first like a mythical "field of dreams."[1] After initial consultation with Howa Construction, Mr. Skaggs selected MHTN Architects, Inc., for project design, and Big-D Construction Company for the work. Groundbreaking took place on August 6, 1997, after which Msgr. Fitzgerald and Dr. Colosimo planted religious medals in various spots of the site, dedicating the work to the heavenly patrons, especially Our Lady of Guadalupe, Saint Joseph, the holy angels, and John the Baptist.

During the following three years, with the support of Mr. Skaggs and his staff, the dream of new schools was transformed into the reality of the Skaggs Catholic Center in Draper, Utah. On December 9, 1998 Bishop Niederauer blessed the 100-foot high lighted cross tower at the center of the campus to confirm the new Catholic presence in Draper. Following the blessing, the diocese hosted a lunch in the shell of the future high school gymnasium for the thousand workers on site. On what was an unusually cold day, Bishop Niederauer addressed the workers in English and Spanish, thanking them for their labor. He invited them to bring their families to see the final product of their work, and reminded them that what was accomplished by the work of their hands would give glory to God, the creator of all that is good.

As the completion of the school buildings neared, Dr. Colosimo was appointed principal of Juan Diego Catholic High School on September 8, 1998, and Sr. Karla McKinnie, CSC, an experienced Holy Cross educator, of St. John the Baptist Elementary School on the following day. A principal for St. John the Baptist Middle School was named in 2000 because of the increased enrollment. Dedication of the center took place on September 26, 1999. Bishop Niederauer celebrated the Mass of dedication, and the Most Reverend William J. Levada, archbishop of San Francisco, was homilist. As the flags were raised on the grassy entrance circle to begin the dedicatory ceremony, trumpets sounded and the Cathedral's Madeleine

Choir School sang. Three thousand people filled the gymnasium. Large television screens enabled them to watch Bishop Niederauer process toward the gymnasium, blessing the grounds and facilities as he approached. There were few dry eyes as the procession entered and the miracle of the Skaggs gift was truly celebrated.

In his homily Archbishop Levada described the "cradle to college" Catholic center at 11800 South 300 East in Draper as a "spacious up-to-date campus . . . (and) an impressive architectural achievement." He continued,

> *But what adds to the visitor's impressions is the iconography and art work, especially the beautiful statues of Christ and the saints, which grace the halls and walls, the common space and the grounds. Our Lady of Guadalupe appearing to Juan Diego is a life-size painted bronze statuary group next to the flags in the entrance circle.*[2]

At the conclusion of the ceremony, Sam Skaggs was invested as a Knight of St. Gregory the Great, and Aline a Dame of St. Gregory the Great, honors bestowed by Pope John Paul II to commend their love for the poor and generosity to the Church. The papal awards acknowledge that, for Sam and Aline Skaggs, "wealth is a gift from God that is to be shared." They remain poor in spirit, avoiding recognition, yet touching innumerable lives by their charity. For them Catholic education is a road to significant achievement for disadvantaged youth.

The Skaggs' commitment to Catholic endeavors has spanned the eras of Bishop Weigand and Bishop Niederauer. Among their contributions have been those to the Cathedral Altar Society in 1980[3], to Catholic Community Services and to Judge Memorial over a period of years. The Skaggs donated their former residence as a home for bishops of the diocese in 1995, financed the restoration of the rose window in the Cathedral of the Madeleine during its interior restoration in the mid-1990s, and annually provide scholarship funds to support needy students in diocesan schools. The deep faith of the Skaggs is known more by their actions than by their words. At the dedication of the Skaggs Catholic Center, Archbishop Levada considered it a pleasure and a privilege to join in honoring Sam and Aline for their extraordinary vision, and their generosity to Catholic education for the benefit of present and future generations.

Italian marble sculpture of the Pieta, dedicated to the Holy Cross Sisters in memory of Bishop Joseph Lennox Federal, graces the grounds of the Skaggs Catholic Center.
PHOTO COURTESY OF DIOCESAN ARCHIVES

A reception and tour of the new complex followed the dedication ceremonies. Utah's Governor Michael Leavitt captured the enthusiasm of the dedication day, exclaiming, "This is truly breathtaking. . . . their (the Skaggs') gift to this valley is staggering. This is a Catholic school complex like none other."[4]

Juan Diego Catholic High School had opened in August 1999, with 300 freshmen and sophomore students, and would expand to include juniors and seniors by the year 2001. St. John the Baptist Elementary and Middle Schools opened also in 1999. The schools house 100 classrooms, state-of-the art science and computer labs, two large libraries, media centers, three gymnasiums, athletic diamonds, basketball and tennis courts, weight rooms and playgrounds for all age groups, performing arts facilities and a 1,350-seat auditorium. Ancillary projects include Vivian Skaggs Armstrong Convent, given to the diocese in 1998 in memory of Sam's mother, and the Guardian Angel Daycare Center completed in 2000. Draper's old St. John the Baptist Mission was sold and a new parish established at the Skaggs Catholic Center. Rev. Terence M. Moore was named its first pastor. He enthusiastically undertook the work of developing parish ministries and oversees construction of what will be one of the finest churches in Utah.[5]

With the first year of school well underway, a time capsule was installed in the wall of the high school central gathering area. The capsule became the storehouse of unique treasures that preserve the history of the new center, and also tell the story of the students' own lives at the turn of the century. The enrollment at Juan Diego Catholic High School during the school year that began in the fall of 2002 topped 700 students; and nearly 1,000 students are enrolled at St. John the Baptist Elementary and Middle Schools.

The heart of Juan Diego Catholic High School is the chapel, which best symbolizes the purpose and ideals of the Skaggs Catholic Center with its commanding stained-glass windows beautifully depicting the apparition of Our Lady of Guadalupe to St. Juan Diego. The windows were crafted by Jenkyn Powell and his son Eli. In the chapel and throughout the complex, original works of art and statuary reflect the traditional Catholic heritage of faith and commitment to learning.

December 9th marked the feast day of (Blessed) Juan Diego, who was later canonized a saint by Pope John Paul II on July 31, 2002 in Mexico City, and in whose honor the new high school is named. Msgr. Fitzgerald and Dr. Colosimo represented the diocese at the canonization ceremony in the grand basilica. St. Juan Diego was a 16th-century Aztec Indian to whom Mary, the Mother of God, appeared in 1531 as Our Lady of Guadalupe, later declared Mother of the Americas. St. Juan Diego epitomizes the poor and marginalized so loved by Sam and Aline Skaggs. The English translation of the saint's Spanish name is "Eagle Who Speaks," and thus a soaring eagle was chosen as the mascot for the high school. The patronage of St. Juan Diego celebrates the common faith and vast diversity of people of all ethnic origins within the schools and the diocese. The saint's genealogy speaks in a special way to Utah's Native American and Hispanic populations, acknowledging the richness that their growing numbers bring to the heritage of the Catholic Church of Utah.

Groups from the diocese, as well as those from neighboring civic communities, regularly benefit from the generosity of Sam and Aline Skaggs in the center's ample and welcoming accommodations for liturgical, educational, athletic, social, and cultural events. It has been said that completion of the new center brings to the diocese its finest hour since the building of the beautiful Cathedral of the Madeleine a hundred years ago. Another "field of dreams" has truly blossomed forth.

NOTES: *The Sale of Utah's Catholic Hospitals (pages 22-29).*

[1] *Salt Lake Tribune*, Edward McDonough, November 28, 1993.

[2] Sister Catherine O'Brien, CSC, President of the Congregation, to the Most Reverend William K. Weigand, Bishop of Salt Lake City, May 17, 1993.

[3] *Salt Lake Tribune*, Cherill Crosby with JoAnn Jacobsen-Wells, November 5, 1993.

[4] Sr. Catherine O'Brien, CSC to Bishop Weigand, May 17, 1993.

[5] Rev. Robert J. Bussen, Vicar General, Consultors' Meeting Minutes, May 18, 1993.

[6] *Salt Lake Tribune*, Crosby and Jacobsen-Wells, November 5, 1993.

[7] Bishop Weigand to His Eminence Eduardo Cardinal Martinez Somalo, Sacred Congregation for Institutes of Consecrated Life, Vatican City State, October 12, 1993.

[8] Bishop Weigand , Memorandum to File regarding Catholic Hospitals, October 15, 1993.

[9] *Deseret News*, Joseph Bauman, November 5, 1993.

[10] Most Rev. Agostino Cacciavillan, Apostolic Pro-Nuncio, Apostolic Nunciature, to Bishop Weigand and Sister Catherine O'Brien, CSC, November 23, 1993.

[11] *Deseret News*, Bauman, November 25, 1993.

[12] *Salt Lake Tribune*, Joan O'Brien, November 25, 1993.

[13] Sr. Patricia Vandenberg, CSC, President and Executive Officer, HCHS, South Bend, IN to Stanley Urban, President, Sisters of Charity Health Care System (SCH), October 18, 1993.

[14] Bishop Weigand, Statement about Holy Cross Healthcare Services of Utah, October 1, 1993.

[15] *Our Sunday Visitor*, Ann Carey, November 28, 1993.

[16] Bishop Weigand Statement, October 1, 1993.

[17] *Intermountain Catholic*, Barbara S. Lee, July 15, 1994.

[18] Msgr. J. Terrence Fitzgerald to Dominic Welch, *Salt Lake Tribune*, August 15, 1994.

[19] Msgr. Fitzgerald, Remarks at Holy Cross Hospital Prayer Service, August 21, 1994.

[20] Msgr. Fitzgerald, Utah Catholic Sale Update, February 26, 1995.

[21] Ibid.

NOTES: *CHRISTUS St. Joseph Villa (pages 29-33).*

[1] Brochure, "Centennial of the Congregation of the Sisters of Charity of the Incarnate Word, 1866-1966," in folder, "Incarnate Word, Sisters of Charity of the."

[2] Mother M. Elizabeth to The Most Reverend Duane G. Hunt, D.D., August 25, 1946.

[3] Brochure, untitled, with photo of new building at address 475 Ramona, undated, ca. 1995.

[4] Villa News, Vol.1, Issue 2, March 1988.

[5] *Salt Lake Tribune*, April 23, 1988.

[6] "Blessing and Dedication of St. Joseph Villa Continuum of Care, April 2, 1995; and Grand Opening Celebration of Additional Services" 8-page brochure.

[7] *Intermountain Catholic*, May 1, 1998, page 1.

[8] *Intermountain Catholic*, June 5, 1959, section 2, page 9.

[9] "Sisters of Charity of the Incarnate Word Golden Jubilee 1947-1997," brochure, March 19, 1997.

[10] *Intermountain Catholic*, April 17, 1998, page 3.

[11] Brochure, "CHRISTUS St. Joseph Villa, 1993-2002"; telephone interview with Ginger Moulton, Development Director, CHRISTUS St. Joseph Villa, August 29, 2002. (See also *Intermountain Catholic*, November 20, 1998.)

[12] Ibid.

[13] Ibid.

NOTES: *Catholic Community Services (pages 33-37).*

[1] CCS Agency Strategic Plan, 1994.

[2] Bishop Joseph Lennox Federal to Dear Monsignor/Father, Sept. 23, 1975.

[3] CCS Community Vision Newsletter, Winter 1995.

[4] *Intermountain Catholic*, November 10, 1989.

[5] *Salt Lake Tribune*, October 21, 1989; November 1, 1989, CCS file.

[6] Original signed certificate, October 7, 1994, CCS file.

[7] *Intermountain Catholic*, January 10, 1992.

[8] *Intermountain Catholic*, March 1, 2002.

[9] *Salt of the Earth*, 1992 ed., the History of the Catholic Church in Utah 1776-1987, Bernice Mooney, pages 426-427.

[10] *Intermountain Catholic*, March 21, 1997.

[11] Ibid., May 28, 1999.

[12] Ibid., June 5, 2001; June 22, 2001.

[13] Ibid., February 1, 2002.

[14] Ibid., April 5, 2002.

[15] *Salt Lake Tribune*, September 7, 2002, by Jacob Santini.

NOTES: *Catholic Foundation of Utah (pages 38-39).*

[1] Archives Finding Aid to records (1985-current year) of The Catholic Foundation of Utah, 1993.

[2] Certificate of Incorporation of CFU in the State of Utah, February 24, 1993.

[3] Bishop Niederauer in "A Foundation for the Future," Annual Report, 1999, page 1.

[4] "A Foundation for the Future," page 1.

[5] *Intermountain Catholic*, January 14, 2000.

[6] "A Foundation for the Future," page 4.

NOTES: *Skaggs Catholic Center (pages 40-46).*

[1] *Catholic San Francisco*, "Ordinary Time," October 1, 1999, pg. 5. Archbishop Levada tells how Bishop Niederauer likened the project to a Catholic school "field of dreams."

[2] *Catholic San Francisco*, page 5.

[3] John Hartman, Pres., Skaggs Companies, to Altar Society Pres., Cathedral of Madeleine, April 2, 1980.

[4] *Salt Lake Tribune*, Christopher Smith, September 27, 1999.

[5] Skaggs Catholic Center *Newsletter*, Vol. 3, Winter 1999. (See also *Intermountain Catholic* special editions, September 24 and October 1, 1999.)

III

THE CHURCH COMMUNITY

Bishop Niederauer has observed ". . . that the Church is the Body of Christ, the People of God, that lay people are its flesh and blood, and the clergy and religious orders are its servant-leaders."[1] Some of the names that surface in recent history as representative of the People of God are recorded below. Also honored, respectfully between the lines, are the unacknowledged men and women among them, the innumerable unsung heroes in every parish, mission, school and agency of the diocese who daily express their faith in quiet lives of selfless service.

DIOCESAN PRIESTS 1988-2002

The lives of three native diocesan priests, Msgr. William E. Vaughan (1908-1988), Msgr. William H. McDougall (1909-1988), and Msgr. Jerome C. Stoffel (1910-2001) provide eyewitness accounts of the story of the Diocese of Salt Lake City during the twentieth century. Msgr. McDougall remembered peeking on tip toes into the coffin of Bishop Lawrence Scanlan (1843-1915) not long after the bishop died on May 10, 1915. Monsignors Vaughan, McDougall and Stoffel graduated from Judge Memorial Catholic High School in the late 1920s. Each of their families personally knew seven of the eight bishops of the diocese.

Msgr. Vaughan was ordained on June 10, 1933. As assistant pastor he played a role in the growth and development of parishes in Salt Lake City, Magna, Ogden and Eureka. And as a chaplain, sometimes concurrently with his parish work, he also lived much of the history of Holy Cross Hospital, the College of St. Mary of the Wasatch, and the University of Utah Newman Center. He worked as a canonist in the Chancery Office for some years, but is best remembered as pastor of Sacred Heart Parish (from 1950 to 1963) and builder of the present Sacred Heart Church. Msgr. Vaughan also oversaw construction of the present church of St. Ambrose Parish where he was pastor from 1963 until his retirement in 1980. His extensive knowledge of the history of the diocese was often reflected in his speeches, writings and photography.

A year after his ordination in 1936, Msgr. Stoffel was assigned to Notre Dame de Lourdes Parish in Price, Utah. Like the missionary priests before him, he brought the sacraments regularly to isolated Catholics in distant corners of southern and eastern Utah when roads were poor and few. During World War II he served as a chaplain in the U. S. Army Corp in Italy and France. Upon his return he was appointed pastor of St. Thomas Aquinas Parish and Newman Center in Logan where he remained for 30 years. He often traveled throughout the state to research the Catholic history of Utah, visiting old mining and railroad camps, or studying petroglyphs on canyon walls, always preserving his findings on film, slides and tapes. Msgr. Stoffel was named the first archivist of the diocese, and was awarded the honor of a Fellow of the Utah State Historical Society. He played a major role in Utah's bicentennial project of retracing the 1776 journey of Dominguez and Escalante into Utah.

When Msgr. McDougall entered the seminary he left behind a colorful career as a newspaper reporter in Wyoming, Utah and, later, Japan. He was writing for United Press International in Shanghai, China in 1941 when the attack on Pearl Harbor sent him in harrowing flight from the Japanese. He crowded onto the *Poleau Bras*, a small Dutch vessel that pushed out into the Indian Ocean, but was soon sunk by machine-gun fire from nine enemy aircraft. He was afloat and alone in the ocean all afternoon before a crowded lifeboat miraculously appeared on the horizon and hauled him aboard. Finally reaching landfall on the southern coast of Sumatra, the exhausted survivors on the lifeboat swam ashore, only to be captured a short time later by the Japanese. They were herded into Palembang Jail, an improvised prisoner of war camp where they remained until the end of the war. They were never officially freed, but, emaciated and weak, they found the gates open and the guards gone on September 19, 1945.[2]

Determined then to dedicate his life to God, Msgr. McDougall was ordained at age 42, and became rector of the Cathedral of the Madeleine from 1960 to 1980. There he worked tirelessly as an "imaginative and resourceful advocate for peace, human life, and the poor."[3] He guided St. Mary's Home for Men, and was active in Traveler's Aid (now known as *The Road Home*), Big Brothers and Big Sisters, and the Right to Life movement. The Utah Press Association honored him with the distinction of enrollment in the Utah Newspaper Hall of Fame on March 13, 1999.

DIOCESE OF SALT LAKE CITY

A profile of the deaths and ordinations of priests serving in Utah: **1988** *to* **2003:**

NECROLOGY	DIED	ORDAINED	DATE
Rev. James R. Garvey	05-20-88	Rev. Gebran Bou-Merhi	06-29-88
Rev. Msgr. Wm E. Vaughan	05-24-88		
Rev. Msgr. W. H. McDougall	12-08-88		
Rev. Francis J. Kunz, CM	06-08-89		
Rev. Gennaro F. Verdi	06-03-91	Rev. Thomas L. Culleton	08-23-91
Rev. Thomas J. Meersman	09-22-91	Rev. Ken. L. Vialpando	08-24-91
Rev. Martin A. McNicholas	01-16-91		
Rev. Joseph H. Valine, OP	09-26-92	Rev. Eugenio M. Yarce	02-22-92
		Rev. Kenneth Beal	05-30-92
		Rev. Albert N. Kileo, ALCP	06-26-92
		Rev. Robert T. Moriarty	06-27-92
		Rev. William F. Wheaton	06-27-92
Rev. Msgr. Francis T. Kelleher	03-31-93	Rev. Javier G. Virgen	09-04-93
Rev. Robert B. Head	11-06-94	Rev. David J. Bittmenn	06-25-94
		Rev. Erik J. Richtsteig	06-25-94
		Rev. Michael R. Sciumbato	06-25-94
Rev. Francis R. LaMothe	04-25-95	Rev. Langes J. Silva	06-03-95
Rev. Msgr. Mark O.Benvegnu	12-17-95		
Rev. Charles E. Freegard	04-09-96		
Rev. William M. Mobley	12-24-96		
Rev. Maurice A. Prefontaine, SSS	08-12-96		
Rev. Paul Kuzy, CPPS	03-27-97	Rev. Gustavo A. Vidal	06-28-97
Rev. Richard S. Blenner, OSFS	06-30-97		
Rev. Anthony Vollmer, CPPS	11-11-00	Rev. Patrick H. Elliott	05-19-00
MOST Rev. Joseph L. Federal	08-31-00	Rev. Richard T. Sherman	05-19-00
Rev. Thos. L. McNamara, OSFS	02-29-00		
Rev. Msgr. Jerome C. Stoffel	05-13-01	Rev. Samuel Dinsdale	05-29-03

PRIESTS AND BROTHERS IN RELIGIOUS ORDERS 1988-2002

In the era preceding the turn of the century, the growing shortage of priests throughout the United States impacted the ranks of religious orders of men serving in Utah. For example, *The Paulist Fathers, CSP* had arrived from their motherhouse in Scarsdale, New York in 1938 to lay the early foundations of today's thriving parish churches in Vernal (1938), Bountiful (1943), and Layton (1947). They established St. Paul Chapel, which served downtown Salt Lake City from 1974 until its closure in 1996. The Paulists maintained the presence of at least two priests in these parishes for a period of fifty years, making a tremendous contribution to the growth of Catholicism in Utah. But in 1988 they reluctantly withdrew from the Diocese of Salt Lake City, because they had no priests available beyond those needed for the order's primary commitments to the fields of communications and evangelization. "This is a painful time," said Fr. Carlo Busby, CSP, first consultor of the Paulists. "We hate to pull back."[4]

In 1931 *Franciscan Friars, OFM* came to Provo in Utah Valley, treading ground visited in 1776 by their forefathers, the missionary-explorers Dominguez and Escalante. Over the following 65 years, 55 Franciscan Friars and Brothers from the Province of Santa Barbara, California imbued the Parish of St. Francis of Assisi in Provo with their spiritual identity, and left an indelible mark on the diocese. However, the dwindling supply of priests led the Franciscan Fathers to the "hard decision" of withdrawing from Utah in 1996. Upon their departure, Bishop Niederauer regretfully bid them goodbye, while also inviting them to return if ever possible. Concelebrating the farewell Mass was Father Finian McGinn, Franciscan vicar provincial, who recalled, "You welcomed us over the years with kindness, understanding and tolerance; you have prayed for us and with us . . ."[5]

Another religious order of men in Utah celebrated a notable anniversary. The year 2002 marked the fiftieth year since the *Jesuit Fathers* arrived in Utah in 1952 from the California Province at Los Gatos, at the invitation of Bishop Duane G. Hunt. They took over administration of St. Henry Parish in Brigham City, and Santa Maria Mission, Ogden which was elevated to the status of St. Mary Parish by Bishop Hunt in 1957. The Jesuits have maintained these ministries to the present time, with Father F. Warren Schoeppe, SJ, serving as pastor since 1986 at Brigham City and its mission of Santa Ana in Tremonton; and Fathers John G. Ferguson, SJ and Martin I. Rock, SJ ministering at St. Mary Parish, Ogden. The order also supplied teachers for St. Joseph Catholic High School in Ogden. The Jesuits now further strengthen and support the diocese with the presence of

St. Francis of Assisi Parish, located in Provo since its 1892 establishment, was moved to a new multipurpose center pictured above in Orem on Ash Wednesday 2000; Father William H. Flegge, pastor. The former mission-style church in Provo, dating back to 1936, is under restoration by the Centro Hispano Foundation. PHOTO COURTESY OF THE INTERMOUNTAIN CATHOLIC

Father Paul J. McCarthy, SJ at St. Thomas More Parish, Sandy; Father Joseph W. Morris, SJ appointed in 1993 as pastor of Good Shepherd Parish in East Carbon City; and of Father Joseph S. Rooney, SJ serving as pastor both of St. Pius X, Moab, and St. Joseph, Monticello since 1998.

Overlooking the circle at Salt Lake's Mount Calvary Catholic Cemetery is a cross, dedicated in 1999 to honor the memory of the deceased bishops of the diocese.
PHOTO COURTESY OF THE INTERMOUNTAIN CATHOLIC

The names of each of the eight bishops (and one auxiliary bishop) are etched on the base of the cross. Two separate headstones mark the graves of the only two diocesan bishops buried at Mount Calvary, Bishop Duane G. Hunt and Bishop Joseph Lennox Federal. PHOTO COURTESY OF THE INTERMOUNTAIN CATHOLIC

Two other orders saw major changes in leadership. *Fathers and Brothers of the Congregation of the Blessed Sacrament, SSS* became associated with the diocese at Sacred Heart Parish and St. Paul Chapel, both in Salt Lake City, from 1981 to 1992. They ministered at St. Patrick, Eureka as well as at St. John Bosco Mission in Delta and Holy Family Mission in Fillmore from 1985 to 1992. Since 1992 they have served at St. Martin de Porres Parish, Taylorsville, where Father Dana G. Pelotte is pastor, and maintained a presence at San Andres, Payson from 1992 until 2002. Also with the Blessed Sacrament Fathers at Taylorsville are Brother David Phelan, SSS, director of religious education at St. Martin de Porres, and Brother James Anthony, SSS, who serves at St. Patrick Parish, Salt Lake City. As the year 2002 drew to a close, the Blessed Sacrament community announced its withdrawal from St. Martin de Porres Parish, due to clergy shortages.

One of the Blessed Sacrament priests, Father Anthony Schueller was director and chaplain of St. Paul Center in downtown Salt Lake City from 1985 until 1991 when he was named a consultor of his order. He became editor of the order's magazine, *Emmanuel*, and in 1995 was elected provincial of the Congregation of the Blessed Sacrament, Province of St. Ann, Cleveland, Ohio. When the Salt Lake contingent of the Blessed Sacrament Fathers and Brothers celebrated the centennial of the founding of the order in November 2000, Father Schueller, provincial, returned to the diocese to join in the ceremonies.[6]

Following the term of Abbot Malachy Flaherty, the 23 Trappist monks of the *Order of Cistercians of the Strict Observance, OCSO*, at the Abbey of Our Lady of the Holy Trinity at Huntsville, Utah, elected Father Leander Dosch as abbot for a six-year term on January 12, 1995. A native of Canada, he had been at the monastery for twenty years, and would lead the abbey into the new century. He was succeeded as abbot by Father Casimir Bernas, a monk and scripture scholar at Huntsville since 1949 who was ordained a priest in 1958. Bishop Niederauer conferred the abbatial blessing in August 2001. Plans for new buildings are underway to replace the three World War II surplus Quonset huts which have served as the main quarters of the monks since they arrived in Huntsville in 1947 from Gethsemani, Kentucky.[7]

PERMANENT DIACONATE
DIOCESE OF SALT LAKE CITY 2002

Director of Ongoing Formation of Deacons: Sr. Jeremia Januschka, OSB, 1998-
Director of Deacon Candidates: Sr. Georgita Cunningham, RSM, 2001-

CLASS OF 2000

Ordained by Bishop George Niederauer on November 19, 2000,
St. George Parish, St. George
Director of Formation: Deacon Owen Cummings, Ph.D.

PERMANENT DEACON	WIFE	2002 ASSIGNMENT
Aguirre, Rigoberto	Maria	Beryl Junction; Christ the King, Cedar City
Davies, Dennis (Denny)	Gail	Christ the King, Cedar City
Gorman, John (Jack)	Barbara	St. George Parish, St. George
Regan, Joseph	Pat	St. George Parish, St. George
Tellez, Rogaciano	Juanita	St. George Parish, St. George

CLASS OF 1997

Ordained by Bishop George Niederauer on November 30, 1997,
Cathedral of the Madeleine, Salt Lake City
Director of Formation: Sister Ellen Mary Taylor, CSC

PERMANENT DEACON	WIFE	2002 ASSIGNMENT
Bourget, Mark A. Sr.	Esther	St. George, St. George
Bulson, Michael E.	Mary Lou	St. Joseph, Ogden
Carranza, Robert	Remon	St. Marguerite, Tooele
Cormier, Joseph H.	Lee	St. Marguerite, Tooele
Godina, Fernando L.	Beatrice	Sacred Heart, Salt Lake City
Huffman, Rick	Gaylynn	Saints Peter and Paul, West Valley City
Johansson, Philip	Ofa	St. Patrick, Salt Lake City
Manu, Sefo A.	Rose Anna	St. Patrick, Salt Lake City

PERMANENT DEACON	WIFE	2002 ASSIGNMENT
Merino, Reynaldo Q.	Margaret	St. Francis Xavier, Kearns,
Mota, Hector	Vita	Our Lady of Guadalupe, Salt Lake City
Rodriguez, Mario	Margarita	Our Lady of Guadalupe, Salt Lake City
Salaz, Rubel J.	Teresa	Hospice, and St. Francis Xavier, Kearns
Spencer, Noel W. (Mick)	Barbara	San Andres, Payson
Stewart, Thomas J.		St. Olaf, Bountiful; and Ogden Regional Medical Center

CLASS OF 1987

Ordained by Archbishop John R. Roach on September 26, 1987,
St. Mary Basilica in Minneapolis, MN

PERMANENT DEACON	WIFE	2002 ASSIGNMENT
Langner, Russell	Wendy	Blessed Sacrament, Sandy

CLASS OF 1981

Ordained by Bishop William K. Weigand on June 6, 1981,
Cathedral of the Madeleine, Salt Lake City

PERMANENT DEACON	WIFE	2002 ASSIGNMENT
Kirts, Steven	Annette	St. Thomas More, Sandy
Sliger, Douglas R.	Terry	Hill AFB – Christ, Prince of Peace Chapel
James McElfresh	Lynn	Retired

CLASS OF 1979

Ordained by Bishop Joseph Lennox Federal on May 17, 1979,
St. Marguerite, Tooele (Deacon Garcia); and on Feb. 21, 1979,
St. Therese, Midvale (Deacon Johnson)

PERMANENT DEACON	WIFE	2002 ASSIGNMENT
Garcia, James D.	Nita	St. Marguerite, Tooele
Johnson, Lynn R.		Cathedral, Salt Lake City

CLASS OF 1977

Ordained by Bishop Joseph Lennox Federal on December 18, 1977,
Cathedral of the Madeleine, Salt Lake City

PERMANENT DEACON	WIFE	2002 ASSIGNMENT
Lopez, Anthony	Connie	St. Joseph, Ogden
Sanchez, Mel	Evelyn	St. Joseph the Worker, West Jordan
Quintana, Robert J.	Sinfrosa	Retired

Ordination of first class of permanent deacons, Cathedral of the Madeleine, December 26, 1976.
PHOTO COURTESY OF DIOCESAN ARCHIVES

CLASS OF 1976

Ordained by Bishop Joseph Lennox Federal on December 26, 1976,
Cathedral of the Madeleine, Salt Lake City

This first class ordained in the diocesan diaconate program marked the 25th
anniversary of its ordination at a celebration in the cathedral on September 9, 2001.
Founding Director of diocesan Permanent Diaconate Program:
Msgr. John J. Hedderman

PERMANENT DEACON	WIFE	2002 ASSIGNMENT
Bambrick, Robert	Pauline	St. Henry, Brigham City
Buller, Thomas		St. Joseph, Ogden
Coniff, John	Lenore	St. Joseph, Ogden
Flaim, Mansueto	Mary	St. Ann, Salt Lake City
Mayo*, Silvio	Mary	Cathedral of the Madeleine, Salt Lake City
Otero, Tranquilino	Stella	Retired
Palm, Lowell	Mary Jane	Our Lady of Lourdes, Salt Lake City
Stott, Stanley	Alice	St. Therese, Midvale
Wardle, Bud		St. James, Ogden
Weis, John C.	Janet	Retired
Werling, Richard E.	Patricia	St. Henry, Brigham City

*Chancellor, Diocese of Salt Lake City, 1985-

DEACONS NOT INCARDINATED IN DIOCESE OF SALT LAKE CITY

Herron, Dan	St. Patrick Parish, Salt Lake City
O'Brien, Jack	St. George Parish, St. George

On August 21, 1994 the Benedictine Sisters formed an independent priory. The sisters later established their residence and ministry at Ogden's Mount Benedict Monastery, dedicated on September 18, 1999; Sister Mary Zenzen, OSB, prioress.

PHOTO COURTESY OF THE INTERMOUNTAIN CATHOLIC

RELIGIOUS ORDERS OF WOMEN DIOCESE OF SALT LAKE CITY 1988-2002

RELIGIOUS ORDERS PRESENT IN YEAR 2002, & YEAR ARRIVED IN UTAH	HIGHLIGHTS OF MINISTRY DURING YEARS 1988-2002
Sisters of St. Benedict, OSB (Mount Benedict Monastery, Ogden UT), 1944	**1988-present:** Assume administration of Our Lady of the Mountains Retreat House, Ogden **1990:** Begin formation of independent priory, later established on Aug. 21, 1994 with 11 Benedictine Sisters **1994-present:** Make transition from St. Benedict Hospital to Ogden Regional Medical Center (after sale of St. Benedict Hospital) **1999-present:** Mount Benedict Monastery dedicated on Sept. 18, 1999
Congregation of the Sisters of Charity of the Incarnate Word, CCVI (Houston TX), 1947	**1988-present:** Begin major expansion of facility and health care at CHRISTUS St. Joseph Villa, Salt Lake City (see also pages 29-33) **1988-2000:** Ministry at St. Anthony, Parish, Helper **1990-present:** Ministry at St. Ann Parish, and at Kearns-St. Ann School
Congregation of the Sisters of the Holy Cross, CSC (Western Region), 1875	**1991:** Celebrate 116 years' ministry in Utah; **1993-1994:** Divest of 3 Holy Cross hospitals (see also pages 22-29)

RELIGIOUS ORDERS
PRESENT IN YEAR 2002,
& YEAR ARRIVED IN UTAH

HIGHLIGHTS OF MINISTRY
DURING YEARS 1988-2002

Congregation of the Sisters of the Holy Cross, CSC
(Western Region), 1875,
continued

1994-present: Establish Holy Cross Ministries, and collaborative ministry with CCS
1995-present: Enter health care ministry at CHRISTUS St. Joseph Villa; ongoing pastoral care at Cedar City, Park City and Tooele
1998-present: Open Women's Welcome Center
1998-present: Holy Cross Ministries opens Midvale office
1998-present: Provide principal and staff for St. John the Baptist Elementary School, Draper
1999-present: Assume office of superintendent of diocesan schools, Pastoral Center
2001: Gather for regional meeting of Holy Cross Sisters at Skaggs Catholic Center

Daughters of Charity of St. Vincent de Paul, DC
(Province of the West, Los Altos Hills, CA), 1920

1992: End 35 years in elementary education at J. E. Cosgriff Memorial School
1995-present: End 35 years at St. Olaf Parish and School; continue Special Needs Scholarship program for Catholic Schools
1998: End Carbon County presence of 71 years; Notre Dame Regional School closed

Discalced Carmelite Nuns, OCD
(Monastery of Carmel of the Immaculate Heart of Mary, Salt Lake City, UT), 1952

1988: Purchase 4 acres land south of monastery
1990: Celebrate bicentennial of founding of Order
1997: Celebrate centenary of St. Therese of Lisieux
1998: Secular order members of discalced Carmelites take vows
2000: Welcome St. Therese of Lisieux relics on world tour
2002: Mark 50th anniversary of arrival in Salt Lake City and establishment of Carmel of Immaculate Heart of Mary

Franciscan Sisters of the Atonement, SA
(Graymoor, Garrison, NY), 1946

1990-present: Continue pastoral care at St. Benedict Hospital (as of 1994 Ogden Regional Medical Center); continue as pastoral associate, then administrator, at St. Joseph the Worker Parish, West Jordan
1990: Left ministry at Roosevelt (begun in 1955) and Vernal to assume role of pastoral associate at St. Marguerite, Tooele (1990-2000)

Members of the Diocesan Youth Group traveled to Rome for World Youth Day in August 2000. Here they visit the shrine of St. Maria Goretti, Netluno. Among those accompanying them were Mary Fasig, diocesan director of Youth Ministry (fifth row, left, in white), and Msgr. Robert R. Servatius (top row). PHOTO COURTESY OF DIOCESAN ARCHIVES

RELIGIOUS ORDERS PRESENT IN YEAR 2002, & YEAR ARRIVED IN UTAH	HIGHLIGHTS OF MINISTRY DURING YEARS 1988-2002
Franciscan Sisters of the Atonement, SA (Graymoor, Garrison, NY), 1946, *continued*	**1998:** Mark arrival of Order in Utah and centenary of founding of Order in U.S. **2001-present:** Director, diocesan offices (at Pastoral Center) of Ethnic Ministry, and Persons with Disabilities
Our Lady of Victory Missionary Sisters, OLVM (Victory Noll, Huntington, IN), 1939	**1991-present:** Retreat ministry at Orangeville, Utah **1999:** End directorship (since 1983) of office of Native American and Ethnic Ministry **2000:** End 17 years of ministry in Moab **2002:** End ministry at Women's Welcome Center in Salt Lake City
Sisters of Mercy of the Americas, RSM (Regional Community of Omaha, NE) 1910-1916 & 1994	**1994-1996:** Ministry at Catholic Community Services **1996-1998:** Holy Cross Ministries, and St. Patrick Parish, Salt Lake City **1998-2000:** Pastoral care at St. Patrick Parish **1999-2003:** Bishop's delegate for Women Religious **2001-present:** Director of Deacon Candidates

RELIGIOUS ORDERS
PRESENT IN YEAR 2002
& YEAR ARRIVED IN UTAH

HIGHLIGHTS OF MINISTRY
DURING YEARS 1988-2002

**Sisters for Christian
Community, SFCC**
(Salt Lake City, UT), 1992

1994-present: V. A. Medical Center, Salt Lake City
1995-2002: Chaplain, Utah State Hospital, Provo
2000-present: Director, Holy Spirit Convent and
House of Prayer, Salt Lake City

**Sisters of the
Holy Family, SHF**
(Mission San Jose, CA), 1953

1988-2001: End religious education and pastoral
care begun in 1983 at St. Mary of Assumption,
Park City and St. Lawrence, Heber
1994-present: Director social/human
services at St. Vincent de Paul Parish,
Salt Lake County
1997: Celebrate 125th anniversary of founding of
Order of Sisters of the Holy Family, SHF

**Congregation of the Sisters of
St. Louis, Juilly-Monaghan,
SSL** (California Region), 1996

1996-present: Director of Diocesan
Spirituality Center

RELIGIOUS ORDERS OF WOMEN
Whose presence in diocese ended during era of 1988-2002:

**Union of the Sisters of the
Presentation of the Blessed
Virgin Mary, PBVM**
(Generalate, County Kildare,
Ireland), 1965-1994

1965-1994: Elementary education; pastoral care
and parish ministry at St. Vincent de Paul
Parish, Murray

**Sisters of Notre Dame,
SNDdeN**
(Ohio Province,
Cincinnati, OH), 1982

1991: End ministry at Brigham City and Tremonton
1992: End ministry in diocesan Office of Hispanic
Affairs; end position (1984-1992) of administrative
assistant to bishop
1992-1993: Doctoral intern at V. A. Medical Center,
Salt Lake City
1992-1994: Ministry at St. Benedict
Hospital, Ogden
1995: End directorship of Blessed Kateri
Tekakwitha Center, Fort Duschesne

RELIGIOUS ORDERS OF WOMEN
Whose presence in diocese ended during era of 1988-2002, continued:

Dominican Sisters, OP
(Adrian, MI & Racine, WI),
1979-1999

1988-1999: Administrator, St. Peter Mission, American Fork
1988-1994: Pastoral care, religious education, immigration services at San Felipe Mission, Wendover
1989: End position of diocesan director of Media Communications

Maria-Cruz Gray, director of the diocesan Office of Hispanic Ministry (standing directly behind those seated, third from right) is shown at a gathering of the Diocesan Hispanic Commission. The group meets regularly to support programs serving the pastoral needs of the Hispanic people throughout the diocese. Bishop Niederauer has significantly increased the number of weekly Spanish Masses and Hispanic ministry for the rapidly growing population. PHOTO COURTESY OF THE DIOCESAN OFFICE OF HISPANIC MINISTRY

PARISH, NEWSPAPER, AND CEMETERY ANNIVERSARIES

Celebrated During 1988-2002:

Year	Parish	Founded	Anniversary
1996	The Cathedral of the Madeleine, pro-cathedral church, Salt Lake City	1871	125 years
2000	St. Joseph Parish, Ogden	1875	125 years
2000	The Cathedral of the Madeleine, laying of cornerstone	1900	100 years
1990	Immaculate Conception, Copperton (originally Holy Rosary, Bingham Canyon)	1890	100 years
1992	St. Francis of Assisi, Provo (now Orem)	1892	100 years
1992	St. Patrick, Salt Lake City	1892	100 years
1988	Our Lady of Lourdes, Salt Lake City	1913	75 years
1992	Sacred Heart, Salt Lake City	1917	75 years
1992	St. Ann, Salt Lake City	1917	75 years
1991	Our Lady of Lourdes, Magna	1916	75 years
1993	Notre Dame de Lourdes, Price	1918	75 years
1997	St. James, Vernal	1922	75 years
2000	St. Therese of the Child Jesus, Midvale	1925	75 years
2000	St. Vincent de Paul, Murray	1925	75 years
1990	St. Helen, Roosevelt	1940	50 years
1991	St. Thomas Aquinas, Logan	1941	50 years
1993	St. Olaf, Bountiful	1943	50 years
1994	Our Lady of Guadalupe, Salt Lake City	1944	50 years
1995	St. Anthony of Padua, Helper	1945	50 years
1997	Good Shepherd, East Carbon City	1947	50 years
1997	St. Elizabeth, Monroe (formerly Richfield)	1947	50 years
1998	St. Ambrose, Salt Lake City	1948	50 years
1998	St. Rose of Lima, Layton	1948	50 years
1998	St. Bridget, Milford	1948	50 years
2000	St. Henry, Brigham City	1950	50 years

Year	Cemetery & Newspaper	Founded	Anniversary
1997	Mount Calvary Catholic Cemetery, Salt Lake City	1897	100 years
1999	*Intermountain Catholic* diocesan newspaper	1899	100 years

LAY MEN AND WOMEN IN COMMUNITY LIFE

Since their earliest days in Utah Catholics have been recognized for their collaboration with fellow citizens on behalf of the common good of the community. In recent years Salt Lake City acknowledged the long and dedicated public service of John W. (Jack) Gallivan by naming its downtown gathering place, the Gallivan Center, in his honor. This welcoming oasis at the center of the business district conveyed the spirit of the 2002 Olympics to the world, and regularly hosts cultural, ethnic and civic celebrations.

The Catholic presence is seeded indiscriminately throughout the common ground of civic life in Utah. Palmer DePaulis was elected to lead Salt Lake City as its 31st mayor during the years 1985-1991. His collaborative style, outreach for the poor, and drive to restore historic buildings had a significant impact on city life. Robert C. Steiner served as a Senator in the Utah State Legislature during terms in which he represented District 3 from 1991-1992, and District 1 from 1993 through 1998. Rod Betit was appointed executive director of the Utah State Department of Health on February 5, 1993, and continues to hold that position today. William D. Hurley directed the Utah State Department of Transportation for a decade ending in the late 1980s.

Among other Catholic officials in local government have been Donna Evans of St. Joseph the Worker Parish, who was chosen mayor of West Jordan in 1997; and Evelyn Nielsen of St. Elizabeth Parish, Monroe who became mayor of Salina, Utah in 1998. Joseph Bonacci, St. Anthony of Padua Parish, was elected mayor of Helper in 2001; and David Armstrong, Notre Dame de Lourdes Parish, Price, was named superintendent of the Carbon County School District. A cathedral parishioner, Darlene Robles, held the position of superintendent of the Salt Lake City Public School District from 1997- 2001.

Midvale City mayor, JoAnn Seghini (St. Therese of the Child Jesus Parish) accepted the "Recognition Award for 2002 Healthier Communities" from the Deseret Foundation on November 14, 2002. Ruben Jimenez served as director of the Utah Office of Hispanic Affairs from 1993 to 1996, and helped focus attention on the many gifts offered the community by people of diverse ethnic backgrounds.

Catholics like Dr. Dominic and Virginia (Ginni) Albo, Irene Sweeney, John and Jean Henkels, the Thomas Kearns McCarthey Family, Rosemary Baron, Rosa Key, Dee Rowland and Judge Andrew Valdez serve on community boards and foundations with distinction. Mary Kay Griffin and Jess Agraz are mayoral appointees to the Board of the Salt Lake City Airport Authority.

For nearly sixty years Richard A. Kane, Past State Deputy, and Master Fourth Degree of the Knights of Columbus, has consistently participated in the Utah State Councils' numerous community-oriented projects, including many in support of human life. The Catholic Woman's League and the Diocesan Council of Catholic Women, currently guided by Sylvia D'Ambrosio and Kathleen M. Jones respectively, provide significant service and support for a variety of civic charities. The Salt Lake Council of Women honored Catholics, Margaret Hearley May in 1988, and Ann Bero and Ida Stonda Brunati in 1998 by electing them to its prestigious Hall of Fame. The list of those who give generously to the cause of Scouting includes Don Ellefsen, Roger and Shirley Mares and S. Al Sonnenburg, to name a few. Since 1978 when the Hibernian Society was incorporated in Utah, the Neville brothers and their families, along with Father Patrick F. Carley, chaplain, have played a major role in the organization.

In Ogden Robert P. and Mary Evans, as well as Allan M. and Kay Lipman, significantly impact the life of the community. The Lipmans also cooperated extensively in the restoration of the historic chapel at Fort Douglas on the east bench of Salt Lake City, for the use of athletes and visitors during the 2002 Olympics, and for continuation of the chapel's long heritage of interdenominational worship. A commercial establishment, the DeBouzek Engraving Company, founded in 1900 by Jean Antonine DeBouzek in downtown Salt Lake City, served the community over the span of an entire century. Following their father's death in 1971, his sons, Paul (d. 1979) and Jean M. DeBouzek who had worked with their father, continued to operate the company until its closure in 1999.

Catholics acknowledge reciprocal cooperation of the interfaith community with their own endeavors. Catholic Community Services, the Madeleine Arts Festival, CHRISTUS St. Joseph Villa, and the three Catholic high schools of the diocese— St. Joseph, Ogden; Judge Memorial, Salt Lake City; and Juan Diego, Draper-- annually honor generous benefactors for their charitable efforts. The inherent Catholic spirit of community service continues to impact Utah's civic life. Within the Catholic Church itself papal honors are awarded to lay men and women, as well as clergy and religious, for extraordinary commitment to the faith.

(next page) In 1996 Judge Memorial Catholic High School marked the 75th anniversary of its establishment in Salt Lake City. Living members of the graduating class of 1929 were honored at the anniversary celebration. An historic photo of the original class of 1929 is seen on the following page.
PHOTO COURTESY OF JUDGE MEMORIAL CATHOLIC HIGH SCHOOL

PAPAL HONORS CONFERRED UPON CLERGY AND LAITY OF DIOCESE OF SALT LAKE CITY, 1988-2002

PAPAL HONOR	DATE	NAME
Protonotary **Apostolic**	April 30, 2001 May 6, 2002	Rev. Msgr. John J. Sullivan Rev. Msgr. J. Terrence Fitzgerald
Prelates of Honor (Reverend Monsignor)	January 13, 1988	Rev. Msgr. John J. Hedderman Rev. Msgr. James T. Kenny Rev. Msgr. John J. Sullivan
	December 5, 1991	Rev. Msgr. J. Terrence Fitzgerald Rev. Msgr. M. Francis Mannion Rev. Msgr. Robert C. Pollock
	February 18, 1994	Rev. Msgr. Robert J. Bussen Rev. Msgr. Robert R. Servatius
	April 30, 2001	Rev. Msgr. Victor G. Bonnell Rev. Msgr. Rudolph A. Daz Rev. Msgr. George F. Davich Rev. Msgr. Francis B. Pellegrino Rev. Msgr. Lawrence P. Sweeney
Order of St. Gregory The Great Knights of the Order	December 4, 1988 July 6, 1998	Sir John W. Gallivan Sir Emerson Sturdevant Sir Sam Skaggs
Dames of the Order	July 6, 1998 August 30, 2000 August 31, 2000	Lady Aline Skaggs Lady Grace Mary Gallivan Lady (Miss) Irene C. Sweeney Lady Jane F. McCarthey
Equestrian Order of The Holy Sepulchre of Jerusalem Western Lieutenancy: Knights of the Order	December 4, 1988	Rev. Sir Neale W. Herrlich, S.J. Rev. Sir Thomas L. McNamara, O.S.F.S.

PAPAL HONOR	DATE	NAME
Equestrian Order of The Holy Sepulchre of Jerusalem Western Lieutenancy: Knights of the Order, *continued*	October 5, 1997	Most Rev. George Niederauer, KC*HS
	October 25, 1998	Sir Robert Majka Sir William Melville
	October 10, 1999	Sir Dominic Albo Sir Emmanuel D. Herbert Deacon Sir Silvio Mayo
	October 1, 2000	Rev. Msgr. Sir Robert J. Bussen Rev. Msgr. Sir J. Terrence Fitzgerald Sir John B. Henkels Sir Norbert Neumann Sir Wayne Stewart Rev. Msgr. Sir John J. Sullivan
	October 7, 2001	Sir Larry J. Cochran Sir Gregory A. Glenn Sir Michael L. Joseph Sir Allan M. Lipman Sir Carmen A. Mancuso Very Rev. Sir Joseph M. Mayo Rev. Sir James Semple Rev. Msgr. Sir Robert R. Servatius Sir Frederick Lewis Strasser Sir Thomas A. Taylor
	October 6, 2002	Sir Lee Budell Sir Michael Herbert Derbidge Sir Dan B. Fuehring Sir Thomas E. La Voie Rev. Sir Terence M. Moore Sir Dennis Terrance Moriarty Sir Timothy Joseph Petracca Sir James P. Seaman Sir Paul D. Slack
Ladies of the Order	December 4, 1988	Lady Enid (Mrs. Walter E.) Cosgriff
	November 23, 1993	Lady (Miss) Irene C. Sweeney
	October 25, 1998	Lady Jo Ann Majka Lady Marilyn Melville

PAPAL HONOR	DATE	NAME
Equestrian Order of The Holy Sepulchre of Jerusalem Western Lieutenancy: Ladies of the Order, *continued*	October 10, 1999	Lady Virginia Albo Lady Mary Mayo
	October 1, 2000	Lady Jean M. Henkels Lady Mary Jeanne Neumann Lady Teresa Stewart
	October 7, 2001	Sister Lady Margo Diane Cain, C.S.C. Lady Diane Cochran Lady Sally Ivers Lady Maury Joseph Lady Nora H. Mancuso Lady Pamela Camille Strasser Lady Pauline Y. Taylor
	October 6, 2002	Lady Mary Teresa Budell Lady DiAnn Kristine Derbidge Lady Lois Ann Fuehring Lady Nancy L. Giles Lady Lynde D. Hoopes Lady Dora Ann La Voie Lady Karen Frances Moriarty Lady Laura Jean Petracca Lady Madalyn Sue Seaman Lady Katherine B. Slack
Order of St. Sylvester Knights of the Order	November 23, 1993	Sir Richard J. Howa Sir M. Ray Kingston

AWARDED THE PAPAL MEDAL, *PRO ECCLESIA ET PONTIFICE*

January 8, 1989

Mother Mary Aloysius Alejo, O. C. D.

Sr. M. Joan Allem, C. S. C.

Sr. Francis Forster, O. S. B.

Sr. Margaret Liam Glenane, S. A.

Sr. Angela Marie Hinckley, S. H. F.

Sr. Annunciata Keogh, P. B. V. M.

Sr. Thecla Mahony, C. C. V. I.

Sr. Lorraine Masters, O. L. V. M.

Sr. Anna Rita Montoya, O. L. V. M.

Sr. Elizabeth Marie O'Connor, C. S. C.

Sr. Germaine Sarrazin, D. C.

Sr. Arles Silbernick, O. S. B.

Sr. M. Clarita Stoffel, C. S. C.

Sr. Stella Marie Zahner, D. C.

April 29, 1989

Mary Bowers

Justine Buller

Mary Cerroni

Henrietta Diamanti

Jeanne Donahoe

Margaret Dowse

Emma Entwistle

Virginia Gillet

Mary Hedderman

Roberta Hunt

Rosa Key

Marion Lipman

Wanda McDonough

Ann Mark

Margaret May

Bernice Mooney

Susan Neilson

Roselee Norwood

Dolores Pennington

Kay Sheehan

Eleanor Smith

Helen Struble

Irene C. Sweeney

Melva Williams

NOTES:

[1] "The Church Listens to Flannery O'Connor," Bishop George Niederauer in paper he presented at BYU symposium, November 10, 1995, page 1.

[2] *Six Bells Off Java* and *By Eastern Windows*, William H. McDougall, Jr., Western Epics, Inc., Salt Lake City, 1948, 1955.

[3] Msgr. J. Terrence Fitzgerald in a public tribute recorded in the *Intermountain Catholic*, July 26, 1996.

[4] *Intermountain Catholic*, November 11, 1988.

[5] Ibid., July 12, 1996.

[6] *Diocesan* and *National Catholic Directories*; *Intermountain Catholic*, November 10, 2000.

[7] Intermountain Catholic, September 7, 2001.

IV

BISHOP
GEORGE H.
NIEDERAUER

EIGHTH BISHOP 1995–

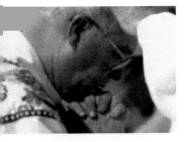

W*hile directing the affairs of the diocese during the early months of the interregnum, Msgr. Fitzgerald, diocesan administrator, also anticipated the arrival of the new bishop, who it was thought would likely be appointed later in the year. On June 1, 1994 Monsignor wrote to the priests, deacons, religious, Diocesan Council of Catholic Women, the Catholic Woman's League and the Knights of Columbus setting the focus of preparations for the arrival and ordination of the bishop-elect. "We will establish committees to begin planning various events . . . (although) our plans are tentative and very dependent on the new bishop and the Pro-Nuncio."[1]*

PREPARATION FOR THE ORDINATION OF THE NEW BISHOP

Msgr. Fitzgerald served as chair of the planning process. The six other consultors, who were significantly involved with him in diocesan affairs throughout the year of interregnum, comprised the coordinating council. They included Msgr. Robert J. Bussen, Msgr. John J. Hedderman, Msgr. M. Francis Mannion, Father Thomas L. McNamara, O.S.F.S., Msgr. Robert R. Servatius, and Msgr. John J. Sullivan. By September lay men and women, clergy and religious had been selected to serve on the varied planning committees. Chair persons were appointed as follows: liturgy, Msgr. Mannion; public social events, Father Joseph M. Mayo; publicity, Dee Rowland; deanery celebrations, Msgr. Servatius; printed programs, Irene C. Sweeney; parish and institutional participation, Father William Wheaton; and hospitality and special services, Msgr. Hedderman.[2] Two major events were projected: first, an evening prayer service of welcome (from both church and civic officials) at which the bishop-elect would present the papal document of his appointment, and receive the blessing of his insignia. The second, to take place the following afternoon, would be the rite of ordination and installation by which he would officially assume the office of the eighth bishop of the diocese.

The ordination of Bishop George Niederauer as eighth bishop of the Diocese of Salt Lake City took place in the Cathedral of the Madeleine on January 25, 1995. Here Bishop William K. Weigand formally greets his successor, Bishop Niederauer.
PHOTO COURTESY OF LYNN R. JOHNSON, THE SALT LAKE TRIBUNE

Despite its limited seating capacity, the Cathedral of the Madeleine was chosen as the site of the celebrations because of its importance for Utah's Catholic history. Supporting this decision was a national trend indicating that "most of the episcopal ordinations and installations taking place in the United States these past couple of years have been in the respective diocesan cathedrals."[3] In the Salt Lake cathedral seating had to be restricted to the bishops in attendance, the bishop-elect's guests, choirs, clergy, religious and other ministers. The fact that only a few seats were available for diocesan and parish groups was mitigated by plans for an evening reception at the Red Lion Hotel at which members of diocesan boards, commissions and councils could meet the new bishop following the ordination.[4] A professional video of the ceremonies was commissioned for later viewing throughout the diocese. In addition, the new bishop would travel to each of the five diocesan deaneries to meet and pray with Catholics during the first weeks of his presence in Utah.

A resource booklet, "A Bishop to Lead the Church," researched and written by the Parish and Institution Committee, enlightened the public prayer, reflection and catechesis during the continuing months of waiting for the appointment of the bishop. The booklet offered insight into ecclesiastical leadership, contemporary Church documents on the ministry of today's bishop, and the history of the local Church. Suggestions were offered for catechetical sessions and parish gatherings. Selections from the ordination ceremony were included for the prayer and reflection of adults as well as children. The booklet greatly enriched the appreciation of Utah Catholics for the role of their bishop as teacher, sanctifier and governor.[5]

Finally, on November 3, 1994, the announcement came that Pope John Paul II had appointed Msgr. George Niederauer of Los Angeles, as eighth bishop of Salt Lake City. The choice of the bishop-elect was known several days earlier by Msgr. Niederauer and diocesan principals, but Church protocol mandates strict secrecy until the date set for formal announcement of the appointment. Msgr. Niederauer arrived in Salt Lake City on Tuesday evening of November 2 and would meet the next day with the diocesan consultors. He offered Mass for the first time in his new cathedral on Thursday morning, delivering his first homily from the cathedral pulpit to the few morning regulars. He later attended noon prayer at the cathedral with some 35 priests, and enjoyed lunch with them in Scanlan Hall.

Within the next week arrangements were in process for the bishop's episcopal ordination. Archbishop John R. Quinn of San Francisco agreed to preside at the Liturgical Reception, scheduled in the cathedral for the evening of January 24, 1995. Msgr. Fitzgerald would officiate there as diocesan administrator. The Most Reverend Agostino Cacciavillan, Apostolic Pro-Nuncio to the United States, confirmed his intent to be present at the liturgy of ordination planned for the afternoon of January 25. His Eminence Roger Cardinal Mahony, Archbishop of Los Angeles, accepted the honor of principal consecrator. He would be assisted by the Most Reverend William J. Levada, Archbishop of Portland in Oregon, and the Most Reverend Tod D. Brown, Bishop of Boise, both of whom, with Cardinal Mahony, were former classmates of Bishop-elect Niederauer in the Class of '62 at St. John's Seminary in Camarillo, California. His classmates presented the bishop-elect a miter as a token of their longtime friendship.

As the weeks flew by committees busily filled in blank lines of prepared drafts of invitations, programs and printed materials, and assembled visitor information packets. Reservations for hotel, dinners, reception, and travel arrangements were completed and confirmed. Music selections were finalized, and choir and liturgy practices moved into high gear. Sketches of designated seating in the cathedral were drawn up. When the days of celebration arrived a master schedule of last minute tasks established time lines for specific responsibilities, and arranged for rehearsals of principal participants.⁶

A dinner for visiting VIPs preceded the Tuesday evening Liturgical Reception on January 24, 1995. In the crowded but hushed cathedral at 7:00 p.m. the first sounds heard were those of three knocks on the main door, and Bishop-elect Niederauer's voice, "Peace to all gathered here." Msgr. Fitzgerald and the consultors met him there and led him into the nave of the cathedral. Accompanied by the voices of the Tongan Choir, the participants began the dramatic procession. The liturgical ministers, knights and ladies of ecclesiastical orders, vested prelates including two archbishops and seventeen bishops, and, finally, Roger Cardinal Mahony and Bishop-elect Niederauer took their assigned places. Msgr. Fitzgerald soon formally introduced the bishop-elect to the assembly, which welcomed him with applause.

In his Tuesday evening homily Bishop William K. Weigand of Sacramento, immediate predecessor of the new bishop, pictured his former flock as a people of "anonymity" and "unsung heroes," who nevertheless persevered in their faith. He spoke of the love and support he received from Utah Catholics and how difficult it had been to say goodbye. Archbishop John R. Quinn of San Francisco blessed the ring, miter and pastoral staff of the bishop-elect in preparation for the rite of ordination the following afternoon. Twelve ethnic communities, each with its own colorful apparel and characteristic dignity, moved forward to present gifts symbolic of their distinctive presence in the common humanity of the universal church. These gifts were displayed at the reception afterwards in Scanlan Hall.⁷

Governor Michael O. Leavitt, President Thomas S. Monson, second counselor of the first presidency of the Church of Jesus Christ of Latter-day Saints, and the Rev. Roger Anderson, president of the Salt Lake Ministerial Association, each pledged friendship and cooperation in gracious words of welcome. Bishop-elect Niederauer responded, identifying himself now as a "born-again Utahn," ready, in the words of his heraldic motto, to serve and to give.⁸

The visitors' schedule for the day of the ordination included a special breakfast for Bishop-elect Niederauer's Los Angeles guests, daytime tours of the city, and a VIP luncheon. Buses picked up the entourage from their hotels to bring them to

Joining the deacons, religious and laity attending the ordination of Bishop Niederauer in the cathedral on January 25, 1995 were 80 priests, 32 bishops, six archbishops and a cardinal, as well as the Apostolic Pro-Nuncio to the United States.

the cathedral at 3:45 p.m. Guests were ushered to their seats, and clergy vested for the ordination and installation ceremony beginning at 4:00 p.m. The entrance procession was even more impressive than the previous evening: behind lay ministers, men and women in religious orders, deacons and over 80 priests of the diocese, there solemnly filed 32 bishops, two abbots, six archbishops, Roger Cardinal Mahony, then the Apostolic Pro-Nuncio to the United States, and finally, Bishop-elect Niederauer. The exquisite music of the cathedral choirs, directed by Gregory Glenn and accompanied by the grand organ and symphonic strings, filled the church. The Pro-Nuncio, Archbishop Cacciavillan, pronounced the papal bull. Archbishop Quinn spoke of Bishop-elect Niederauer as the symbolic "watchman" who keeps careful vigilance over his people and listens to them attentively. The bishop-elect then prostrated himself before the altar, as all knelt to sing the Litany of the Saints.

Special respect was paid to retired diocesan bishop, the Most Reverend Joseph Lennox Federal, now in frail health, as fellow priests assisted him in the ceremony of the laying of hands on the bishop-elect. Later, Bishop Niederauer moved across

*During his ordination Bishop Niederauer
kneels to receive the traditional gesture of the
laying on of hands by brother bishops, including
retired Bishop Federal, sixth bishop of the diocese, seen at the center of this photo.*
PHOTO COURTESY OF THE DESERET NEWS

the sanctuary to receive Bishop Federal's symbolic kiss of peace. Following the prayer after Communion, the co-consecrators led the newly-ordained bishop out of the sanctuary into the nave and side aisles of the church, where he blessed the people as he processed along. A hymn of thanksgiving, brief remarks by Cardinal Mahony and Bishop Niederauer, and the solemn blessing ended the rite of ordination.[9]

Visitors later testified to the magnificence of the ceremony. Bishop Joseph M. Sartoris, Auxiliary Bishop of Los Angeles in the San Pedro Pastoral Region, exclaimed:

> *It truly was a glorious day for your Diocese, and a great credit to all the*
> *hard work and beautiful planning that was done. . . I was impressed by the*
> *Cathedral, the music, the splendid ceremonies, the gracious hospitality and*
> *all that you gave to us.*[10]

Roger Cardinal Mahony, Archbishop of Los Angeles, commended Msgr. Fitzgerald,

> *. . . for the marvelous manner in which you hosted the Liturgies of Ordination for*
> *Bishop George H. Niederauer. From the moment that we stepped from our*
> *airplane all the way to our departure, it was very impressive experiencing the*
> *warm hospitality of your outstanding committees . . . I know that all of this*
> *excellence in preparation and arrangements is due to your own personal*
> *leadership, and . . . the wonderful manner in which you carried out all of the*
> *celebrations with such friendliness and good spirit.*[11]

Bishop Niederauer himself expressed thanks to committee members:

> *I appreciate the ease with which you responded to every situation no matter*
> *how difficult. That particular kind of graciousness and seeming effortlessness*
> *can only come from days and months of very hard work.*[12]

The rite of ordination officially terminated the period of interregnum. The year 1994 had closed out a triumphant century of growth in the diocese and laid the groundwork for transition into a new millennium. It was also a year of recapitulation, an assimilation of painful changes shaped by the progress of time and communal history. There was the crushing loss of Utah's three Catholic hospitals; and the ending of the church's ministry from 1974 to 1996 in downtown Salt Lake City when central city redevelopment forced the closure of St. Paul's Chapel and Catholic Center. Also, the departure in 1999 of the Daughters of Charity of St. Vincent de Paul from Price, in a changing school environment, ended 70 years of Catholic education at Notre Dame Regional School there.

But fresh new directions appease the losses of the past: the establishment of the Skaggs Family Foundation for Roman Catholic and Community Charities, the

planting of seeds for the Skaggs Catholic Center, the expansive spirit of Catholic Community Services, the innovative vision of CHRISTUS St. Joseph Villa, the strident success of the Catholic Foundation of Utah, and the enthusiastic beginnings of Holy Cross Ministries. So too the 1991 establishment by Carmen and

Msgr. Fitzgerald, diocesan administrator, dedicated the new church and parish center of St. Rose of Lima, Layton in 1994. Less than four years later the pastor, Msgr. Victor G. Bonnell, and parishioners retired their debt. The church's steeple, topped with a cross, towers above the Layton landscape. PHOTO COURTESY OF DIOCESAN ARCHIVES

Nora Mancuso of the new Mancuso's Religious Goods, Gifts and Books, Inc., continued to provide an abundance of Catholic resources formerly available at the downtown Catholic Center.

As Msgr. Fitzgerald carried out the work of the diocese during his term as administrator, his own history became more deeply identified with that of the diocese. Among his official acts was the dedication of new church buildings at San Felipe, Wendover, St. Helen, Roosevelt, and Our Lady of Perpetual Help Vietnamese Community, Kearns, as well as St. Peter, American Fork and Our Lady of the Snows, Alta. A note that appeared late in 1994 in the weekly bulletin of St. Rose of Lima Parish, Layton, expressed the feelings of the entire diocese: "We all owe an enormous debt of gratitude to Msgr. J. Terrence Fitzgerald who has been the diocesan administrator . . . He has done an outstanding job, and we pray that he will be abundantly blessed for his dedication and service."[13]

THE MOST REVEREND
GEORGE H. NIEDERAUER, Ph.D.

Eighth Bishop of the Diocese of Salt Lake City

Bishop-elect George Niederauer held a press conference at the diocesan Pastoral Center in Salt Lake City on November 3, 1994, the day of his appointment to the diocese. He would be ordained bishop on the following January 25, the Feast of the Conversion of St. Paul, the Apostle of the Gentiles, who traveled extensively teaching the Christian faith. "I realize that I am a California transplant," the bishop-elect said, " but I take heart in the fact that the Catholic Church is by nature missionary and universal . . . now it is my time to go from one place to another proclaiming the Good News, and I welcome this call." The vita of the bishop-elect's life traces the lifelong development of his faith commitment. The early years might suggest the influence of Renaissance scholar Leonardo Bruni: "Let your study be . . . in the skill of letters and . . . in those things which pertain to life and moral character. These . . . perfect and adorn a human being."[1] For Bishop Niederauer's homilies, addresses, writings and conversation regularly reflect his learned familiarity with the humanities.

During the 32 years following his ordination to the priesthood in 1962 Bishop Niederauer ministered as educator, parish priest and seminary rector in the Archdiocese of Los Angeles. In retrospect, this seemingly idyllic sojourn of his life prepared him well to leave the comparatively quiet "Nazareth" of his youth and enter into his public life as Bishop of Salt Lake. He commented to a friend that, "Perhaps by complicating my life in final years, the Lord is simplifying my spirituality, if I let Him."[2]

Following the announcement of the appointment of Bishop-elect Niederauer, letters of congratulation, that flowed into the Pastoral Center in Salt Lake from all over the United States, indirectly witnessed to his life and character. They showed he was highly respected as a teacher, priest and spiritual director: "I have always heard such marvelous things about you, your ability to teach about and communicate spiritual values," wrote Archbishop James P. Keleher, Archdiocese of Kansas City in Kansas on November 16, 1994. A former student wrote, "My own ministry as a priest owes a great deal to your dedication to the Faith and to seminarians, and for this, I am most grateful."[3] A note from Father Michael McCullough of Burbank, California dated December 3, 1994 read, "Your wit, insight and vocabulary have never ceased to amaze me. Thank you for putting your gifts to the service of the Church and God's people." Colleagues of the newly-named bishop testified to his effectiveness as a church leader; one wrote, "You have enriched and enabled all you have served with your caring and visionary leadership."[4]

The warmth of the bishop-elect's associations with lay men and women throughout the Archdiocese of Los Angeles was also apparent—well over 300 friends from California came to Salt Lake City to join in his ordination ceremonies. Afterwards, several visitors expressed "a sinking feeling knowing we all were leaving you there."[5] Having heard of a heavy snow storm in Utah, a friend from Camarillo wrote assuring the new bishop that, "There is no doubt in anyone's mind that you are worthy of the challenges ahead—pastoral, ecumenical, or blizzardous."[6]

Friends and associates portrayed a leader already experienced in the work of teaching, governing and sanctifying. But the ceremony of ordination on January 25, 1995 revealed more:

> It was a most solemn occasion . . . the assembly prayed over the new
> bishop, put his episcopal robes on him, adorned him with his new ring,
> fitted on his miter, handed him his crosier . . .
>
> Then came time for the man himself to respond to the colorful festivity . . .
> of pomp and ceremony. So the new bishop stepped up to the microphone.
> And looking out over his glasses . . . and noting that his flock was
> becoming eerily quiet and motionless, he dryly said, "I sure hope nothing
> falls off."
>
> The flock burst into spontaneous laughter, ratifying by gentle applause
> what they had been hoping: The bishop is human![7]

Bishop Niederauer is by temperament lighthearted. He realizes comic wit can be dark and destructive, but believes it also can be gentle. His innate and sensitive humor gives "things a sense of proportion and keeps them in perspective."[8] Following a two-year initial residence at the cathedral rectory, the bishop established his official residence in the home donated to the diocese by Sam and Aline Skaggs. A self-declared "people person" he often welcomes visitors to his home with gracious hospitality, and hosts meetings of various diocesan groups. "Extroverts are energized," he says, "by being with people." He has a manner of

To begin the Liturgical Reception on the evening of January 24, 1995, Bishop-elect Niederauer knocked three times on the entrance door of the cathedral, calling to those within, "Peace to all gathered here." Msgr. Fitzgerald and the diocesan consultors led him into the nave of the cathedral to be greeted by the awaiting assembly. PHOTO COURTESY OF LYNN R. JOHNSON, THE SALT LAKE TRIBUNE

personal kindness and consideration that somehow empowers both individuals and groups. When his schedule permits some recreation, he reads, plays bridge with friends, enjoys the symphony and movies, or listens to classical music.[9] But his work is clearly cut out for him, and his responsibilities are demanding.

When first appointed, he announced that his highest priority was to be fully present to the priests, deacons, religious, and lay men and women of Utah as their spiritual leader. As soon as possible he met and prayed with the priests, deacons and sisters. The week following his ordination, he embarked on a month-long schedule of visits to become acquainted with the people in Utah's five diocesan deaneries, embracing 43 parishes and 19 missions. But unexpectedly on February 9 he was hospitalized in Salt Lake. "How disappointing this must be for you in your first fervor and with so much percolating on the stove . . . ," wrote a friend from Los Angeles when he heard the news.[10]

Two and one-half weeks later the bishop answered him: "Actually I think I got off easily: one angioplasty, with no heart damage and a stern and effective warning about diet, exercise and stress. I am trying to heed that lesson."[11] This openness and positive attitude are characteristic of Bishop Niederauer even during times of trial and uncertainty. He is a man of quiet strength. By late February he resumed his introductory tour of the diocese. This initial enthusiasm has only expanded with time. The bishop is always on the move, visiting parishes from one end of the state to the other, present for Confirmations, anniversaries, school plays, and community socials. In every place he affirms the goodness of the human spirit. Under his guidance ministries have been developed, and parish, school and mission facilities have been expanded.

BISHOP GEORGE NIEDERAUER

Year	Born
1936	Born June 14, 1936 in Los Angeles, California, the only child of George H. Sr. and Elaine Sullivan Niederauer, both now deceased

Year	Education
1946-1950	Attended St. Catherine's Military Academy, Anaheim, California
1954	Graduated from St. Anthony's High School, Long Beach, California
	Completed freshman year at Stanford University, California

Year	Education, *continued*
1955	*Entered the seminary system of the Archdiocese of Los Angeles*
1959	Earned Bachelor of Philosophy Degree, St. John Seminary, Camarillo, California
1962	Earned Bachelor of Sacred Theology Degree at Catholic University of America, Washington, D.C.
1962	Earned Master's Degree in English Literature at Loyola University, Los Angeles
1962	*April 30: ordained to the priesthood for the Archdiocese of Los Angeles, California*
1966	Earned Ph.D. in English Literature, University of Southern California
1978	Earned diploma from Focus on Leadership program of Theological and Scriptural Studies and Spiritual Direction at Loretto Heights College, Denver, Colorado

Year	Ministry
1962-1963	Assistant Pastor, Our Lady of the Assumption Parish, Claremont, California
1963-1965	Priest in Residence, Holy Name of Jesus Parish, Los Angeles, California
1965-1979	Full-time Instructor of English Literature at St. John Seminary College, Camarillo
1967-1974	Instructor, English Literature, Mount St. Mary College, Los Angeles, summers
1976-1979	Part-time Instructor of Spiritual Theology, St. John Seminary, Camarillo
1979-1987	Full-time Instructor, Spiritual Theology, St. John Seminary Theologate, Camarillo
1979-1992	Part-time Instructor of English Literature, St. John Seminary College, Camarillo
1968-1977	Chairman, English Department, St. John Seminary College, Camarillo
1972-1979	Spiritual Director, St. John Seminary College, Camarillo
1979-1994	Spiritual Director, St. John Seminary, Camarillo
1987-1992	Rector, St. John Seminary, Camarillo
1992-1994	Co-director of Cardinal Manning House of Prayer for Priests, Los Angeles
1984	*Named a Prelate of Honor (Monsignor) by Pope John Paul II*
1994-	*November 3: Named eighth bishop of the Diocese of Salt Lake City*
1995-	*January 25: Ordained bishop in the Cathedral of the Madeleine, Salt Lake City*

UTAH CATHOLIC CHURCH EXPANSION
1994 to 2002:

SITE OF EXPANSION	LOCATION	YEAR BLESSED/ DEDICATED
Our Lady of the Snows Chapel	Alta	**1994**
St. Helen Parish Parish Hall	Roosevelt	1994
St. Peter Parish Social Hall	American Fork	1994
St. Rose of Lima Parish Church and Parish Center	Layton	1994
CHRISTUS St. Joseph Villa Ambrose Wing *Social/Dining Area Expansion*	Salt Lake City	**1995** 2002
Our Lady of Lourdes Parish Church Renovation	Magna	1995
St. George Parish Kuzy Hall *Church Expansion*	St. George	1995 2000
St. Vincent De Paul Center William K. Weigand Resource Ctr.	Salt Lake City	1995
St. Vincent De Paul Parish Chapel of Adoration *Holy Family Center*	Salt Lake City	1995 2001
Blessed Sacrament School Library Addition	Sandy	**1996**
St. Christopher Parish Vollmer Parish Center	Kanab	1996
St. Francis Xavier Parish Rectory *School Hall Renovation*	Kearns	1996 *1999*
St. Ambrose Parish Vaughan Parish Center *Kearns McCarthey Center*	Salt Lake City	**1997** 2002

SITE OF EXPANSION *continued*	LOCATION	YEAR BLESSED/ DEDICATED
St. Mary of the **Assumption Parish**	Park City	
New Church		1997
New Parish Center		*2001*
Skaggs Catholic Center	Draper	
Vivian Skaggs Armstrong Convent		**1998**
Guardian Angel Day Care Center		*1999*
St. John the Baptist Elementary *and Middle Schools*		*1999*
Juan Diego Catholic High School		*1999*
St. James Parish	Vernal	
Bell Tower		1998
Mt. Benedict Monastery	Ogden	**1999**
St. Ann Parish	Salt Lake City	
Kearns-St. Ann School Restoration		1999
Gathering Space Addition		*2002*
Our Lady of Lourdes	Salt Lake City	
School Computer Lab		**2000**
Sacred Heart Parish	Salt Lake City	
Center		2000
St. Francis of Assisi Parish	Orem	
Center		2000
St. Joseph Parish, Ogden	Ogden	
Elementary School Addition		2000
St. Patrick Center		*2002*
St. Therese of the Child Jesus	Midvale	
Religious Education Center		2000
San Felipe Parish	Wendover	
Parish Center		**2001**
Church Renovation		*2002*
Former Chancery	Salt Lake City	
Restoration (S. Temple Red Building)		**2002**
Renamed after *Bishop Duane G. Hunt*		

SITE OF EXPANSION *continued*	LOCATION	YEAR BLESSED/ DEDICATED
Madeleine Choir School New Campus	Salt Lake City	2002
St. Joseph Parish, Monticello New Sacristy	Monticello	2002

PARISHES AND MISSIONS

Established 1994-2002:

PARISH	YEAR-MISSION OF	YEAR ERECTED PARISH
St. John the Baptist, Draper	1981 Blessed Sacrament, Sandy	1999
St. Peter, American Fork	1969 St. Francis of Assisi, Provo	2000
San Felipe, Wendover	1985 St. Marguerite, Tooele	2000
Our Lady of Perpetual Help, Kearns	1986 Utah's Vietnamese Community	2000
MISSION		
St. Sylvester, Escalante	1998 Christ the King, Cedar City	
San Paulo, Beryl Junction	2001 Christ the King, Cedar City	

DIOCESAN CONSTRUCTION PROJECTS UNDERWAY AT END OF 2002

CHRIST THE KING PARISH Church, Center	Cedar City
OUR LADY OF PERPETUAL HELP Church, Center	Kearns
ST. JOHN THE BAPTIST PARISH Church, Center	Draper
ST. JOSEPH CATHOLIC High School Fine Arts Center	Ogden

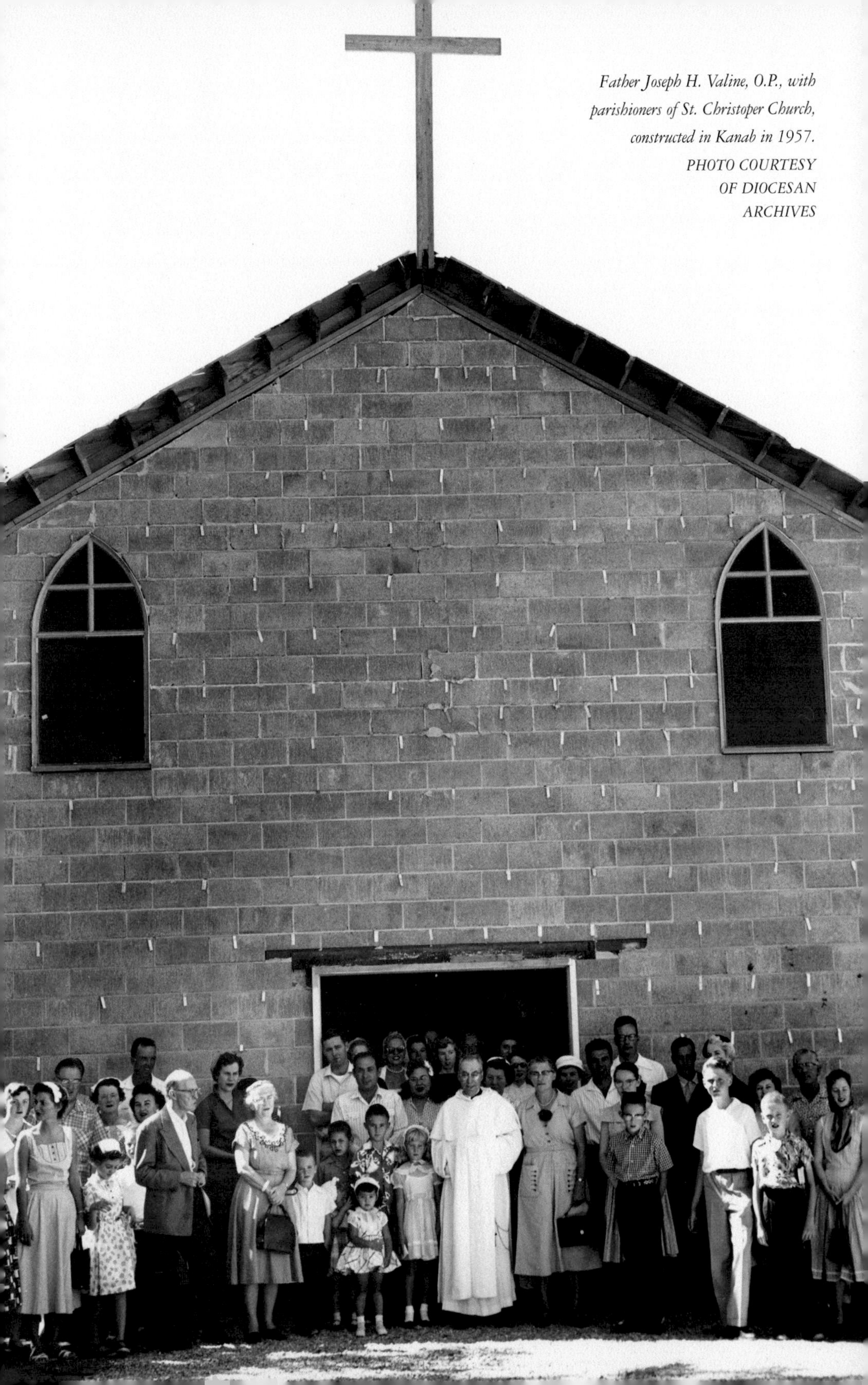

Father Joseph H. Valine, O.P., with parishioners of St. Christoper Church, constructed in Kanab in 1957.
PHOTO COURTESY OF DIOCESAN ARCHIVES

BISHOP NIEDERAUER IN THE DIOCESE AND CIVIC COMMUNITY

Bishop Niederauer determined that the enhancing of Catholic school education would be another priority of his episcopacy. He gave wholehearted support to the proposed Skaggs Catholic Center complex in Draper, Utah which would encompass a parish, a day care center, and elementary, middle and high schools. He considered the groundbreaking ceremony on August 6, 1997 a moment of great hope and resolve.

> *I'm confident that history will point to this gathering as a significant moment in the development of the cultural and educational life in Utah . . . I cannot adequately express in words our appreciation to Sam and Aline Skaggs and their family members for this project, and especially to you, Michael Miller (Skaggs' CEO) and all the people . . . who have given so many hours and days, and so much attention and enthusiasm to this undertaking . . .*[12]

Whether through his columns in the *Intermountain Catholic*, his weekly Sunday homilies at the cathedral, Pastoral Directives, press releases, interviews or media presentations, the bishop addresses current pastoral issues of the day. He provides guidance for the faithful on subjects ranging from the liturgical implementation of the New Roman Missal, sacramental practice, and Cyberspace and the family, to assisted suicide, handgun policy, death penalty or stem cell research. He personally speaks at innumerable civic and social gatherings with humor and relevance. His sessions are always popular at the annual Pastoral Congress held at the Skaggs Catholic Center.

The bishop enthusiastically supports youth ministry. For several years sizeable delegations from diocesan youth programs traveled to World Youth Day with Pope John Paul II and to other national gatherings. A teacher at heart, Bishop Niederauer remains very much at ease during informal discussions with students. He enjoys being back in the classroom; for example, in December 2002 he taught three classes in senior theology at Judge Memorial Catholic High School one day, and a senior literature class at Juan Diego Catholic High School another day. He has also participated in educational programs at Brigham Young University, Provo, and at Salt Lake's University of Utah.

In anticipation of projected population growth in coming years, and to assure an ever stronger Utah Catholic presence in the future, Bishop Niederauer directed

In 1996 Judge Memorial Catholic High School marked the 75th anniversary of its establishment in Salt Lake City.
PHOTO COURTESY OF JUDGE MEMORIAL CATHOLIC HIGH SCHOOL

the diocesan Property Office to seek out and purchase adequate sites, either for enlarging existing parish facilities or establishing new ones. Sites for future development have been acquired in Heber City, Kamas, Ephraim, Hurricane, Beryl Junction, Escalante, St. George, Erda, Monticello, Huntsville, and Tremonton as well as other areas of potential growth throughout the state.[13]

But Bishop Niederauer typically focuses his efforts on core issues, such as the critical shortage of priests. During the late 1990s the diocese implemented a three-year National Vocation Strategy, raising awareness of the challenges and need for vocational recruitment. Other ongoing efforts continue to encourage vocations, and increase the ranks of the fourteen men presently preparing for the priesthood. In the meantime, the bishop is conservatively implementing Sunday Celebrations in the Absence of a Priest in specific situations where the need is pressing and designated ministers are properly prepared.[14]

Often other important issues arise and demand immediate attention. For example, in September 2000, misinformed criticism by some in the community of

(upper) St. George Parish in St. George, Father Wayne T. Epperley, CSSp, pastor, has expanded along with the steady growth of the parish family since its establishment in 1958 in a small duplex. The original building, remodeled in 1979, was reconstructed in 1991 to again enlarge the church of Spanish mission style. (lower) The adjoining Kuzy Hall, named after Father Paul S. Kuzy, CPPS, pastor, from 1984 until his death in 1997, was built in 1995.

PHOTOS COURTESY OF THE INTERMOUNTAIN CATHOLIC

the newly published Vatican document, *Dominus Jesus,* demanded a strong response by the bishop: "Nowhere does the document say that only faithful Catholics can attain full salvation from earthly sin. One of the oldest lies about Catholics is that we believe only Catholics go to heaven . . . *Dominus Jesus* does not criticize or demean interreligious dialogue or ecumenical activity or the agreements and initiations that result from such dialogue."[15]

In a similar incident the following year, Bishop Niederauer quieted a potentially volatile matter regarding the validity of Mormon baptism by immediately clarifying the issue in question: "This is an internal church decision to guide our sacramental practice and that's really all it is." His official statement of July 16, 2001 read:

> On Monday, July 16, 2001, the Congregation for the Doctrine of the Faith
> in Vatican City issued a Responsum ad Dubium (a reply to a question
> submitted to the Congregation) stating that the Baptism administered in the
> Church of Jesus Christ of Latter-day Saints in not valid, i.e., is not to be
> regarded by Catholic pastors as effecting the same Christian initiation which
> Catholic baptism effects.

> Practically and pastorally this response means those former members of the
> LDS Church who are received into the Catholic Church will receive the
> Sacrament of Baptism . . . The practice of the LDS Church of baptizing all
> its new members previously baptized in any other church indicates that the
> LDS Church regards its own baptism as accomplishing something
> substantially different from that of all other baptismal rites . . .

> The declaration of the Congregation for the Doctrine of the Faith should
> not be understood as either judging or measuring a spiritual relationship
> between Jesus Christ and members of the LDS Church. Furthermore
> (as the Responsum states), 'Catholics and Mormons often find themselves
> working together on a range of problems regarding the common good of
> the entire human race. It can be hoped therefore that through further studies,
> dialogue and good will, there can be progress in reciprocal understanding and
> mutual respect.'

Ecumenical activity remains a primary goal of Bishop Niederauer. He notes that:

> (T)he Catholic Church recognizes that in many ways she is linked with
> those who, being baptized, are honored with the name of Christian . . .
> there are many who honor Sacred Scripture, taking it as a norm of belief and
> action, and who show a true religious zeal . . . in some real way they are
> joined with us in the Holy Spirit, for to them also He gives His gifts and
> graces, and is thereby operative among them with His sanctifying power.[16]

When living in California the bishop participated in the Episcopal Church
Spirituality Program, *Amicitia*. He presently continues an active role as a member

of the executive committee of the National Board of the Religious Alliance Against Pornography, and locally as president of the Utah Coalition Against Pornography. He supports the work of Utah's Interfaith Hospitality Network, and the Conference for Community and Justice (which held its annual Thanksgiving service at the Cathedral of the Madeleine on November 13, 2002). In 1999 Bishop Niederauer attended the second annual interfaith convocation of the Freedom Festival in Provo as the keynote speaker at the event.

The bishop has been named a Paul Harris Fellow of the Rotary Foundation of Rotary International "in appreciation of tangible and significant assistance given for the furtherance of better understanding and friendly relations among people of the world." He speaks before many groups, varying from the national prayer luncheon at the Ogden Air Logistics Center, to the meetings of the 96th Regional Support Command of the U.S. Army Reserve in Salt Lake, the Utah Peace Officers, and the Kiwanis as well as other local groups.

A volunteer member of the Utah State Centennial Committee in 1996, the bishop subsequently addressed state gatherings over the years, offering the invocation at the inaugural ceremony of Governor Michael O. Leavitt in 1997, and leading prayer before the Utah State Senate and House of Representatives. In the field of politics, he sees "Compromise as a necessary component of politics in a diverse society . . . Political idealism seeks to make the state a better servant of its citizens; religious faith seeks to make the church a better servant of its believers."[17]

Bishop Niederauer served as a member of the Utah Quality Growth Public-private Partnership, and from 1997 through 2000 of the Coalition for Utah's Future. He now belongs to the Salt Lake City Alliance for Unity. This group of state government officials, religious leaders, editors of the two major daily newspapers, and civic organizers began meeting in early 2001 to address the perceived divisiveness existing between people at all levels of Utah society. The mission statement of the Alliance for Unity expresses a unified effort to bring all people together for the common good. The theme and tone of the statement suggests Bishop Niederauer's full participation in the writing:

> We seek to help build a community wherein differing viewpoints are
> acknowledged and valued. Differences need to be aired, and problems
> resolved in an atmosphere of courtesy, respect and civility . . . Our overriding
> goal is to help people cross boundaries of culture, religion, and ethnicity to
> better understand and befriend one another.[18]

(top & bottom left) Bishop Niederauer formally dedicated a new wing at St. Joseph Elementary School in Ogden on March 19, 2000. The wing provides 12 new classrooms, a computer lab and music rooms. Future phases of construction will add a chapel, gymnasium, cafeteria and offices as well as additional classrooms. (bottom right) At St. Joseph Catholic High School in Ogden construction is underway on a new Fine Arts building that will provide new programs for the school. The center, located north of the existing structure, is scheduled for completion in August 2003. PHOTOS COURTESY OF THE INTERMOUNTAIN CATHOLIC

From 1999 through 2001 parishes throughout the diocese carried out the RENEW program of group study and prayer in celebration of the Great Jubilee Year 2000. At the conclusion of the annual Chrism Mass of 1999 Bishop Niederauer presided over the sealing of two Holy Doors at the mother church of the diocese, the Cathedral of the

(above) St. Mary of the Assumption, Park City, Msgr. Robert J. Bussen, pastor, constructed a parish center, dedicated in August 2001 by Bishop Niederauer. PHOTO COURTESY OF THE INTERMOUNTAIN CATHOLIC

(far left) In 1994 Our Lady of Perpetual Help Vietnamese Community, Kearns, Father Dominic Thuy Dang Ha, pastor, purchased a former LDS stake center and remodeled it into a church. Pictured is the dedication by Msgr. Fitzgerald later that same year. The complex was named a parish in 2000. PHOTO COURTESY OF DIOCESAN ARCHIVES

(left) By 2002 the growth of the Vietnamese parish required major expansion. PHOTO COURTESY OF THE INTERMOUNTAIN CATHOLIC

Madeleine in Salt Lake City. Those doors, and others in designated parishes, would remain closed in anticipation of the arrival of the Jubilee Year. On the eve of the turn of the century the bishop led a solemn vigil during which the sealed Holy Doors were symbolically opened with procession, prayer, and at midnight the singing of the church's great hymn of praise, the Te Deum. The following February three Utah missions were elevated to parish status, celebrating the past growth of the Church in Utah and its promise for the new millennium.

During the Jubilee Year preparations were also underway for the Catholic community, believed to number close to 200,000 or 8% of the state's population,[19]

Efforts by the diocese to acquire the Donald Stromquist property at the southwest corner of First Avenue and C Street were underway in late 2002 and completed early the following year. The diocese thus secured ownership of the entire city block comprising the Cathedral of the Madeleine and diocesan center. Bishop Lawrence Scanlan purchased the original section of the block in 1890.
PHOTOS COURTESY OF THE INTERMOUNTAIN CATHOLIC

The former diocesan Chancery Office was refurbished and named the Bishop Hunt Center in 2002. PHOTOS
COURTESY OF THE INTERMOUNTAIN CATHOLIC

to welcome the world at the Salt Lake City 2002 Olympic Winter Games. Some 46 representatives of 22 religious faiths met for over a year to plan chaplaincy services for the athletes and visitors, and to set the stage for respectful and peaceful games. This Interfaith Roundtable sponsored a pre-Olympics concert January 28, 2002 in the Cathedral of the Madeleine.

Innumerable Catholics served as volunteers on the myriad Olympic projects. A number of Catholics, including Msgr. Robert J. Bussen and Msgr. J. Terrence Fitzgerald, were honored to be among the hundreds who carried the Olympic torch through Utah spreading its motto, "Light the Fire Within." Catholic hospitality centers were set up at six parishes nearest to the Olympic venues in Salt Lake, Huntsville, Kearns, Ogden, Park City and Provo to serve the thousands of visitors. "The whole world comes together for an event like this," said Bishop Niederauer. "It celebrates the aspirations of human beings—the cooperation as well as competition."[20] For the Wasatch Front, the Olympics brought expanded transportation, new facilities and recreational developments. For the Catholic Church of Utah the Olympics provided an opportunity to demonstrate the warmth and zeal of theCatholic embrace.

In March 2002 a scandal of clergy sexual abuse of minors arose in the national Church, bringing the diocese a most trying challenge, despite the fact that it has faithfully implemented its sexual abuse policy since enactment of the policy in May 1990. In June 2002 Bishop Niederauer reviewed diocesan records of the 400 priests who served in the diocese over the past fifty years, and found that there were allegations of sexual abuse of minors in eight cases. In line with his policy of openness with the news media, Bishop Niederauer called a press conference on June 11, 2002 to announce that five of the eight were no longer permitted to function as priests. The other three against whom no allegations of misconduct had arisen following their completion of treatment many years ago, were removed from their current assignments, not to be reassigned.

The diocesan sexual abuse policy, in which all staff and employees of the Diocese of Salt Lake City are well instructed, was revised on August 1, 2002 to incorporate the "Charter for the Protection of Children and Young People," a document completed in June by the United States Conference of Catholic Bishops (USCCB). Bishop Niederauer participated in the writing of this charter. "Nothing is more important than the care of children and the healing of those who have suffered abuse," he said.[21]

In accordance with this charter, the Diocese of Salt Lake City established a Diocesan Review Board in August 2002 to review every case or allegation of abuse of children or young people by priests, deacons or other church personnel. Rosemary (Mrs. Bruce) Baron, principal of Salt Lake's Rose Park Northwest Middle School, was selected to chair the nine-person board representing a cross section of social, legal, health, law enforcement and educational disciplines in the community. Pam (Mrs. John) Sanders, MS, director of administration services of Odyssey House, serves as vice chair. Msgr. J. Terrence Fitzgerald, vicar general, is the delegate of the bishop to the board. Other board members include Deacon Michael Bulson, an attorney with Utah Legal Services; Lt. John Cribbs of the Salt Lake City Police Department; Dr. Penny (Mrs. Ken) Jameson, clinical psychologist; Sr. Jacinta Millan, CSC, an early childhood educator with Holy Cross Ministries; Judge James Sawaya (ret.) of the Third District Court; and Father Colin F. Bircumshaw, Promotor of Justice in the diocesan Tribunal. Staff members serving the board include Monica Howa-Johnson, assistance coordinator and communications director; and Michael Lee, Diocesan Pastoral Operations.

The group met for the first time on September 5, 2002 to establish its bylaws, discuss implementation of the Bishops' Charter, and make its own compelling call to bring about healing and reconciliation. The board commended the clarity and openness of the existing diocesan policy and practice regarding sexual abuse.[22]

During this turbulent chapter in history, Bishop Niederauer is a wise and articulate presence among his fellow bishops in the United States Conference of Catholic Bishops (USCCB). He previously served the Church on the Vatican Visitation Team for Theologates as well as on a number of committees of the USCCB, as follows:

Past member, Bishops' and Presidents' Committee

Consultant, Bishops' Committee on Hispanic Affairs, 11/96-11/99

Committee on Communications; Subcommittee on Standards/Policy,
 11/96-11/99; 11/02-11/05

Committee on Priestly Life and Ministry, 1997-2000

Chairman, Priestly Formation Committee, 11/99-11/02

Member, Administrative Board, 11/99-11-02

Chairman, 2000 Ad Hoc Committee on Nomination of Conference Officers

Member, Budget and Finance, 02/00-11/02

Ad Hoc Committee on Clergy Sex Abuse, 2002.

Bishop Niederauer is a member of the National Federation of Spiritual
Directors, holding the office of president from 1975-1977, and belongs to Alpha
Sigma Nu, the Jesuit Honor Society, in the Loyola Marymount University Chapter.
It is no wonder that his warm, outgoing personality, humor, spiritual perceptiveness
and literary background make him a much sought after director for clergy retreats
throughout the United States. Under the banner of the motto on his coat of arms,
"To Serve and to Give," Bishop Niederauer makes the power and presence of
God's love most visible.

NOTES: *Preparation for the ordination of the New Bishop (pages 76-83).*

[1] Msgr. J. Terrence Fitzgerald to Priests, Deacons, Religious, Diocesan Council of Catholic Women, Catholic Woman's League, and Knights of Columbus, June 1, 1994.

[2] Diocesan Ordination/Installation Planning Committees, revised December 5, 1994.

[3] Msgr. Fitzgerald to Priests, Deacons, Religious, Diocesan Council of Catholic Women, Catholic Woman's League, and Knights of Columbus, June 1, 1994.

[4] Msgr. Fitzgerald to Diocesan Boards/Commissions/Council Members, December 23, 1994.

[5] *A BISHOP TO LEAD THE CHURCH, the Diocese of Salt Lake City Welcomes Its New Shepherd,* William F. Wheaton, Diocesan Director of Religious Education, Editor; and members of the Parish-Institution Preparation Committee, including Father Robert Moriarty, Father J. T. Lane, SSS, and Sister Genevra Rolf, CSC; Diocese of Salt Lake City, November 1994.

[6] Master Schedule of Events and Responsibilities, January 24 and 25, 1995.

[7] List of ethnic groups and gifts, January 27, 1995.

[8] Program, The Liturgical Reception of the Most Reverend George Niederauer, Bishop-elect of Salt Lake City, January 24, 1995.

[9] Program, The Ordination of the Most Reverend George Niederauer as Eighth Bishop of Salt Lake City, January 25, 1995.

[10] Bishop Joseph M. Sartoris, Auxiliary Bishop of Los Angeles, San Pedro Region, to Msgr. J. Terrence Fitzgerald, January 27, 1995.

[11] Roger Cardinal Mahony, Archbishop of Los Angeles, to Msgr. J. Terrence Fitzgerald, January 30, 1995.

[12] Bishop Niederauer to Molly G. Dumas, Catholic Community Services, February 6, 1995.

[13] Weekly parish bulletin, St. Rose of Lima Parish, Layton, Utah, November 27, 1994.

NOTES: *Bishop Niederauer (pages 84-106)*.

[1] Quoted by Dean of College of Humanities, University of Utah, in a letter of November 2002.

[2] Bishop Niederauer to Rev. Harry Thiel, Hmong Catholic Center, Thailand, March 1, 1995.

[3] Rev. R. Clements, Director of Vocations, Diocese of Phoenix, Phoenix, AZ to Bishop-elect Niederauer, November 10, 1994.

[4] William H. Sadlier Dinger to Bishop-elect Niederauer, January 15, 1995.

[5] Robert and Rosalie Hutton, Camarillo, CA to Bishop Niederauer, February 16, 1995.

[6] Mrs. Charles Faulders, Camarillo, CA to Bishop Niederauer, March 3, 1995.

[7] *The Priest*, May 1996, page 25, author unlisted.

[8] Doug Robinson, *Deseret News* senior writer in a wide-ranging interview of Bishop Niederauer published August 19, 2002 in the *Deseret News*.

[9] Ibid.

[10] Rev. Van A. Wagoner, Sts. Peter and Paul Church, Tucson, AZ to Bishop Niederauer, March 3, 1995.

[11] Bishop Niederauer to Father Wagoner, March 21, 1995.

[12] Remarks at groundbreaking of Skaggs Catholic Center, August 7, 1997.

[13] *Intermountain Catholic*, January 14, 2000, page 5.

[14] Bishop Niederauer to Priests of the Diocese of Salt Lake City, November 12, 1997.

[15] *Salt Lake Tribune*, Opinion Section, September 24, 2000, page AA5.

[16] *Lumen Gentium*, Dogmatic Constitution on the Church, No. 15, a document of the Second Vatican Council.

[17] Bishop Niederauer paper on religion and politics, KCPW broadcast at Hinckley Institute, University of Utah, January 23, 1996.

[18] Bishop Niederauer to Pastors and Administrators, September 19, 2000.

[19] *Extension*, January 2002, page 8.

[20] Ibid, page 20.

[21] "The Diocese of Salt Lake City Addresses the Issue of Clergy Sexual Abuse," June 11, 2002.

[22] *Intermountain Catholic*, September 6, 2002.

ILLUSTRATIONS